Preface

Coming up with a preface, I believe, is harder then writing the book. I am a few pages away from sending this book to my publisher and as of today, have no preface or any ideas for one. But, thanks to the book Gods above, they sent me my preface today. While on vacation this week from my nine to five, I decided to take a trip to the St. George Research Library, in hopes of finding a story or two to round off this book. Taking my usual seat at the microfilm machine, I begin my quest. With the machine warmed and all ready for action I set sail into the past. After spending two hours fighting with those old microfilm machines, I get up, return the films to the librarian and head for the door. Before I could exit, I overheard two librarians talking. The conversation grabbed hold of my ears, it went something like this " I didn't realize that Christina Aguilera was born on Staten Island". This was something I knew about, since I wrote a book titled "Famous People from Staten Island". As I turned to set this librarians query straight, to my complete surprise, he was holding a copy of my book. Being as humble as I am, I had to introduce myself as the author. I asked him if he had bought the book and he replied "no, it's a library copy".

To say, I walked out of that library with a smile on my face is a huge understatement.

And so you see , there are many more reasons then financial to write a book and thank the Lord I am not in it for the money. I, as many authors before me have found out, it is much easier writing a book then selling one.

This book is the product of many people who throughout the last few years have shared their stories with me. Three people in particular need some special thanks. Paul A Sharrott, shared his memories with me in the story on Staten Island Moonshine. Kim Kowalczyk shared with me a tale called The Lady in Blue and Don Dolan related his adventures with Eccentric Mr. Organ.

A few of the stories have been taken from some old Staten Island history books.

Staten Island Folklore

Staten Island Folklore

Table of Contents

Preface..1
Staten Island Folklore.................................8
Dueling on Staten Island............................12
The Mad Monk..28
The Lost Guggenheim Treasure..................32
Lucky Luciano...36
Ralph Waldo Emerson...............................42
Treasure Stories..46
The Cost of Guilt.......................................62
The Wrath of a Young Damsel....................68
The Indian Lady..72
Ichabod Crane..84
Lady in Blue 92
Palace Theater...100
Nazi War Prisoner 106
Queen Elizabeth II 114
The Lindbergh Baby..................................118
Indian Caves 122
German Submarine..................................128
The Eccentric Mr. Organ...........................136
Willie Sutton..148
"Mind the Light, Kate"..............................154
The Manhattan Project.............................164

Staten Island Folklore

The Great Bronze Column 174
The Legend of Cropsey...............................184
Who Invented the Telephone?....................190
Sunday Bomber...196
Staten Island Moonshine............................200
The Buried Guineas....................................210
Mr. Bang the Flower Man............................216

Staten Island Folklore

Merry Christmas from Clint

Keep Staten Island in your heart!

John Gains Sublett

Staten Island Folklore

Staten Island Folklore

Like the sale of Manhattan to Dutch settlers for $24, it is a historical legend that has been repeated time and again: Staten Island became part of New York rather than New Jersey, the story goes, because of a sailing contest in the 17th century.

Staten Island Folklore

The tale, long a part of local lore, gained currency at a news conference in Prospect Park, where the Brooklyn borough president, Marty Markowitz, playfully challenged Mayor Michael R. Bloomberg to a pedal-boat race "for the right to call Brooklyn a city again."

Mayor Bloomberg, who firmly rejected the possibility that Brooklyn might again be its own city, as it was before 1898, said, "Staten Island is part of New York, rather than New Jersey, because of just such a race."

Local legend states that Staten Island was associated with New York instead of New Jersey due to the outcome of a wager on a sailing race around the island. Legend has it that when New York and New Jersey competed for ownership of Staten Island, Captain Billopp in 1676 secured Staten Island for New York by circumnavigating the island in one day, thereby giving all islands in the bay to New York. The final adjustment of the boundary between the states of New York and New Jersey was made by a boundary commission after the Revolution and presumably included Liberty and Ellis Islands.

The legend is told to visitors to the Conference House, the house Captain Billopp built in

Tottenville in the 1670s, according to a volunteer at the house.

A mayoral spokesman, said that the legend was "a story the mayor has heard many times from Staten Islanders, and one he recalls reading about for years and years."

The tale was repeated by J. J. Clute's "Annals of Staten Island" (1877) and Cornelius G. Kolff's "A Short History of Staten Island" (second edition, 1926).

Staten Island Folklore

Staten Island Folklore

Dueling on Staten Island

Staten Island Folklore

In a hollow southwest of Black Horse Inn, New Dorp, many gallants and rufflers of the eighteenth century fought their duels with sword or pistol, as the challenged might elect. General Robertson, of the British army, killed a French naval officer, Vollogne, who had resigned his commission and followed him to America for the express purpose of fighting him. General Skinner, of the British army, went out to exchange shots with a Hessian officer, but on General Howe's peremptory order

Staten Island Folklore

he had to defer the duel, and met his death in battle. Two other of Howe's officers, Colonels Illig and Pentman, fought here on horseback for an hour, slashing at one another like savages, and stopping only when they were weak with loss of blood. Major Andre was Illig's second.

Black Horse Tavern on Richmond Road

ORIGINAL SIGN OF THE
BLACK HORSE.

Staten Island Folklore

THE BLACK HORSE TAVERN

All those of General Howe's staff who could not be cared for at the Rose and Crown were quartered at the Horse.

The fireplace nearly dominated the entire west wall. The second floor consisted of one apartment known as the ballroom. The sleeping quarters were back of the bar. The Black Horse Tavern was erected in 1754 and until 1776 was known as Wayside Rest. In 1776 it was occupied by members of the staff of Sir William Howe, one of whom was thrown against a large rock caused by his stumbling horse and was killed. The horse was black and noted as the fastest in the British Army, and because of the incident the name "BLACK HORSE" was applied.

That part of Richmond Road from the Black Horse tavern to and through Richmond Village was formerly known as Stapleton Avenue: this name appears on a map of the property as early as 1854.

Staten Island Folklore

THE NEW DORP DUELLING GROUND.

Almost directly west of the old Black Horse Tavern, at New Dorp, stands a cluster of venerable trees, and on the south side of which is a graceful knoll, known as Camp Hill. Behind this hill - or, rather, to the west of it - is a hollow, which was, a century or more ago, surrounded by dense woods. Far more than a score of duels have been fought at this spot.

Staten Island Folklore

Camp Hill was so named by the British, during their encampment at New Dorp, and its delightful situation soon made it a resort for the officers of that army. Indeed it soon became a miniature "Monte Carlo," and witnessed the ruin of many a promising member of the King's army.

Gambling and dueling in those days were practiced to such an extent as to threaten general demoralization to the royal troops. Sir William Howe repeatedly summoned his generals in council in the "Rose and Crown," his headquarters, with a hope that means could be effected to break up these nefarious practices. Nearly fifty officers were court-martialed and dishonorably dismissed during the encampment of the British army at New Dorp, in consequence of gambling and dueling.

The fact became notorious at one time that even general officers so far lost their dignity and their regard for military discipline that they sat down to the gambling table with private soldiers, and even servants, so great was their greed for money; while, once beyond the shadow of Camp Hill, they would exact the severest discipline and all the bowing and saluting and mimicry that military etiquette demands.

The story has been told of a young Scotch

officer who, after losing all his money on Camp Hill, requested a loan from his rival at the gambling table, in order that he might meet an obligation on the following day, and, on being refused, went alone to the secluded ravine beyond and gave up his life in disgrace.

Colonel Christopher Billopp is said to have had an " honorable encounter " with General Erskine on this ground, neither of whom were injured. Afterward they became the warmest of friends.

The only duel known to have been fought by "plain citizens." on the New Dorp ground, was between young Hamilton and Lathrop. It is presumed that this was the son of Alexander Hamilton, who finally died in a duel at Weehawken, on the identical spot, but prior to, where his father was shot in 1804. Lathrop was an English lawyer, who had come to this country in the interest of Tory claimants.

The romance of this dark spot is told of two line officers belonging to a Highland regiment, encamped at New Dorp. Two officers of a Scottish regiment who sleep side by side in the cemetery of St. Andrew's, Richmond, in forced or seeming friendliness, fell on this ground, each by the hand of the other. They had learned to love a

Staten Island Folklore

fair Staten Island girl, who had become a belle among the officers at the post, as her father was a volunteer aide-de-camp on the staff of Sir William Howe. Whether she showed a preference for either of these hot-headed Highlanders, to the rage of the slighted one, or whether they fought in sheer exasperation because she would notice neither, was and is unknown. They had learned to hate each other with the same intensity that they loved the girl. Friends interceded, after it was learned that a challenge had been given; but neither would give way. They met, with so much anger in their hearts, that they could not be persuaded to clasp each other's hand before the fatal moment to fire arrived. Their seconds, two fellow officers, paced off the ground and then placed a heavy dueling pistol in the hand of each. When all was in readiness each second stood in front of his principal and pleaded for a reconciliation. "We are determined to fight!" was the only response. Then the seconds stepped aside and the fatal word was given. Both fell, mortally wounded; both died in the course of a few days and their remains were laid away in the old Dutch cemetery at Richmond. Their graves, which were side by side, were never marked; but they were long kept green by the same hand the

Staten Island Folklore

two nameless duelists had died to gain. Was the girl smitten with remorse? A slender figure was often seen at twilight in the graveyard where they rest beneath unmarked mounds, and while she lived, those little heaps of earth were kept green and fair. An aged Staten Islander, who knew this lady well when she had grown very old, and was childish and feeble, said that he had repeatedly heard her tell the story of the lovers of her youth, and that she firmly believed that some day one or the other would come back and claim her for his bride.

~ American myths and legends 1903, Volume 1 by Charles Montgomery Skinner

At the commencement of the present century, when what is now Twenty-first street, in New York City, was far out in the country, and was known by no other name than " Love lane," reaching from shore to shore, and lined on either side by great elm trees, it was the scene of many a wicked duel. One of these, however, was planned to take place at New Dorp, but a severe storm prevented it at the time designated. When the parties had got together again they were

Staten Island Folklore

disappointed in the arrival of the barge which was to bring them down the bay to Staten Island, and so the seconds selected " Love lane."

Aaron Burr and Alexander Hamilton are known to have visited New Dorp and to have stopped at the Rose and Crown, on more than one occasion, between the close of the Revolution and the end of the century. They were both firm believers in the very popular idea of that day, that " a duel was an affair of honor," and that it was the proper means by which gentlemen should settle their personal difficulties, instead of going into court and being subjected to the "law's delay." They certainly knew all about the dueling ground at the foot of Camp Hill, and it seems reasonable to assume that they, too, have visited the spot and beheld the peaceful scene, which had been desecrated by those whose sad errors were committed long ere their own should shock the world.

Who knows but that the distance over the restless waters of the bay, on that memorable July morning, in 1804, is alone responsible for preventing the occurrence at New Dorp of those scenes which must forever darken the name of Weehawken Heights, and fill with regret and sorrow and pity the heart of every American citizen which appreciates the noble qualities which Burr and Hamilton both possessed? Unlike any other duel ever fought in the land, both fell—one to his grave and the other in the estimation of his countrymen.

We have endeavored to learn the date of the last duel fought at New Dorp, and are convinced that it was the one in which "young Hamilton and Lathrop" participated, which was probably about 1790; and that it was the only one fought here after the departure of the British army from Staten Island. So it may be classed as almost exclusively a military dueling ground.

A short distance from Camp Hill is an old well and the brush-covered remnant of the foundation of a house. We have been informed by old citizens, who have been familiar with these surroundings for upward of seventy years, that the scene has witnessed no change within their recollection; and more than one has expressed the belief that those relics mark the site of one of the historic structures that stood there during the exciting days of the Revolution..

Though the next duel we write about took place in New Jersey, one of the famous participants actually lived out his last days on Staten Island. The Burr–Hamilton duel was a duel between two prominent American politicians, the former Secretary of the Treasury Alexander Hamilton and sitting Vice President Aaron Burr, on July 11, 1804.

At Weehawken in New Jersey, Burr shot and mortally wounded Hamilton. Hamilton was carried to the home of William Bayard on the Manhattan shore, where he died at 2:00 PM the next day.

Years after the duel, Burr returned to New York City to practice law and was tried and acquitted for his role in the duel. He died in 1836 at Port Richmond in Staten Island, never having apologized to Hamilton's family.

Staten Island Folklore

Staten Island Folklore

St, James Hotel, Port Richmond - where Aaron Burr Died

Staten Island Folklore

Staten Island Folklore

The Mad Monk

Staten Island Folklore

St. Augustine Monastery – During the 1800s, St. Augustine was a holding ground for nuns, priests, and monks in training. Legend states that about sixty years ago a group of monks lived here in solitude and silence, one of the monks went crazy and began to systematically butcher the other monks one by one, dragging them down to the sub-level floors (some people say they go down thirty floors), where the monk's living quarters were located so that he could mutilate their bodies undisturbed and undiscovered, until he was ready to go up and drag down yet another victim.

Eventually his evil deeds were discovered, and he was caught and imprisoned in a cell at one of the lowest levels of the Monastery, where he spent the rest of his days tearing at the walls and wailing like a wounded animal, The story continues to say that if you make it all the way down to the very last level at night, you will see the ghosts of all the murdered monks, as well as hear the screams of the mad monk in his cell spiraling through the halls. I don't know of anyone who has ever ventured that far down, but one person claimed to have made it three levels down only to find a cell-like room whose walls were covered with long, gouged scratch marks and bloody hand prints; the overwhelming sense of terror that gripped this person upon seeing this cell caused him to flee, panic-stricken, up and out of the Monastery. He says he will never set foot near the place again.

Staten Island Folklore

Staten Island Folklore

The Lost Guggenheim Treasure

Staten Island Folklore

Tales of shipwrecks, sunken treasure and pirates has fascinated many a man both young and old. But to hear of one such treasure off the shores of our beloved island, is a dream come true. In 1903, a barge carrying silver and lead traveled passed Port Mobil on the southwest shore of Staten Island. This cargo had come from the Mexican mines by way of Galveston and was on its way from the East River waterfront headed to the American Smelting and Refining Company.

On the still, moonlit night of September 26, 1903, a tug urged the barge Harold out of what's today South Street Seaport and south past the Statue of Liberty. The Harold's load that night was nearly 7,700 silver-and-lead bars. They were destined for Perth Amboy, New Jersey. The silver, and the smelters, belonged to the Guggenheim family, which had made its fortune in mining and smelting.

The cargo never arrived, at least in one batch. Somewhere in the Arthur Kill tidal strait the Harold tipped, sending most of the silver bars to the bottom. The barge's deckhands—"dumbest skunks I ever had to do with," the salvage company's owner later told the New York Times—didn't notice until docking at dawn. A secret salvage effort recovered about 85 percent of the bars, but that still left up to 1,400 "pigs" unfound, from an area between New Jersey and Staten Island known as Story Flats. The value of the remaining 15 percent of the silver was estimated to have been between $10 and $20 million, but in 1980 valued at between $80 and $100 million.

Three competing groups sought rights to salvage the cargo of the barge Harold, which sank in the waters of Arthur Kill during rough seas.

Staten Island Folklore

Staten Island Folklore

Lucky Luciano

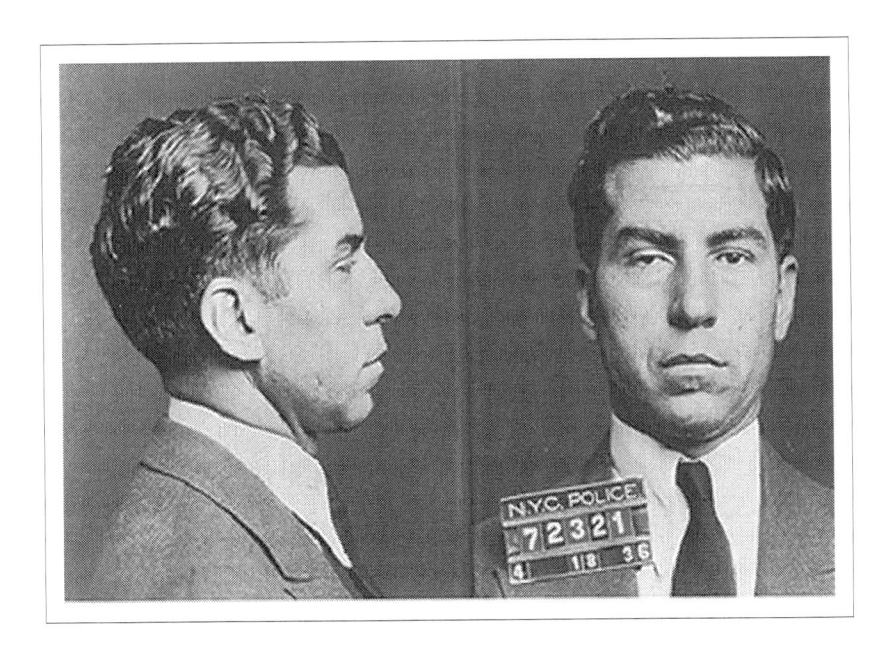

Underworld legend has it that on October 17, 1929, Charles Lucania (later changed to Luciano) was found stumbling along Hylan Boulevard on Staten Island at 1:00 AM. His face was a bloody mess, his eyes were swollen so bad he he could hardly see. His throat had been slashed. He had been taken on a one-way ride in the back seat of a car, thoroughly beaten and left on a wooded field for dead. When he awoke from the terrible beating, he could not believe he was still alive and just wanted to get back to Manhattan. The first person he happened upon, he yelled to them to get him a taxi.

The person he yelled to, turned out to be a patrolman and he was taken to the 123rd Precinct station, where a surgeon from Richmond Memorial Hospital was summoned to treat Lucky's wounds.

Detectives visited the location of the crime which was about eight hundred feet from the Terra Marine Inn and when they searched the area they found small pieces of adhesive tape and a bandage saturated with blood.

He became the rare gangster to survive a "one-way ride"; he was abducted by four men in a car, beaten and was left on a Staten Island beach, but he survived. Luciano was on a dock at on the Hudson River inspecting a load of fresh

Staten Island Folklore

chiba that had just arrived. Four of rival mob boss Salvatore Maranzano's men rolled up in a car, grabbed Luciano and taped his mouth shut. They beat him for an hour as they slowly drove towards Staten Island. Once there, they slit his throat from ear to ear, stabbed him repeatedly with an ice pick, then dumped him in a ditch and left him for dead.

    Lucky Luciano lived through this attack, earning him the nickname "Lucky." Luciano saw the attack as a sign that the gang war had to end, and soon.

    His extensive wounds included a knifing of his face, thereafter causing his right eye to droop.

Staten Island Folklore

Staten Island Folklore

Staten Island Folklore

Ralph Waldo Emerson

Staten Island Folklore

Ralph Waldo Emerson was a regular visitor to the island, his brother William living there and serving as county court judge.

About 1837 County Judge William Emerson purchased the Peter Wandel farm, which included what is now known as Emerson Hill. He repaired and occupied the farmhouse, which was known as The Snuggery. This was situated at the foot of the hill where it swings back from the road. After residing here for a time he built the stuccoed house that stands halfway up the hill. The Walter Price house on the hilltop was erected by Mr. Folsom, the law partner of Judge Emerson. Judge Emerson came from Concord, Mass., and it was he who renamed the locality Concord. His brother, Ralph Waldo Emerson, was a frequent visitor in his house. He is said to have prepared some of his lectures and to have composed many of his poems here. Henry D. Thoreau lived with the Judge's family during the summer of 1843 as a tutor.

Mr. David J. Tysen recalls being taken, when a boy, by his father to call on Judge Emerson, the two being on intimate terms. He describes the Judge as a splendid specimen of manhood, both physically and mentally. On one such occasion he was entertained by Ralph Waldo, and for

Staten Island Folklore

some reason not now remembered he [the boy] quoted in a somewhat grandiloquent tone: "A little learning is a dangerous thing." "Yes, young man," responded Ralph Waldo, "but it is not half as dangerous as to think you know it all."

~ from Legend of Richmond Road – 1916

There was a school named after him on the island
Ralph Waldo Emerson Elementary School PS 12

Staten Island Folklore

Staten Island Folklore

Treasure Stories

New York Tribune October 30, 1921

Staten Island Folklore

*The house at Richmond, Staten Island, built in 1752,
which gives up buriedtreasure periodically*

Staten Island Folklore

Daniel Wandels Farm . . .

On the eastern side of the road, from about Clove Road to Fingerboard Road, lay the Dan Wandel farm. Fifty years or more ago—no one seems to know just when or why or how the story was started on its travels—much excitement was created by a rumor that some of Captain Kidd's treasure was buried here. No one has been found who has seen the color of the Captain's gold, but there are those who recall the story.

~ from Legend of Richmond Road – 1916

Daniel Wandel, a lifelong Staten Island resident, was an old time farmer. In the 1890s he lived in a small stone house at the junction of Richmond and Fingerboard Roads at Concord. When Wandels mother had passed on some thirty years earlier, it was said that she had left a considerable fortune behind.

Before her demise, Mrs. Wandell told her son that after her death he would discover money buried on the farm. With mom well cold in her grave, Daniel gave search for her fortune. With the farm looking like gophers had attacked, he found zilch, nothing, nada.

As time went by, the search for the fortune had ceased until one fateful Friday. The construction workers from Midland Electric Company were working on a trolley pole. They were digging a hole on the road, besides the fence of Wandells property. Daniel was outside watching the men digging. When the excavating was done he spotted an old tin box at the edge of the hole. Keeping quiet so the men would not notice he waited patiently until they had all gone home. He then began digging around the box so as to free it from its resting place. The box was just too heavy for him to lift so a call to his daughter for help rang out. When they succeeded in freeing the box they brought it directly to the kitchen.

Mr. Wandell could hardly contain his excitement. With the prying open of the box came the sight of gold pieces, of every denomination. The entire family was summoned to the kitchen where the coins were carefully counted. The tally was a cool $10,000, in those days this was a fortune.

News of the "Pot of Gold" traveled fast around the neighborhood and they were inundated with well wishes, curiosity seekers, and many new found friends. It may not have been Captain Kidd's Gold but it sure made one island family smile.

When a local news reporter came by for an interview, Wandell refused to make any statement and said he did not care to have the story published.

A number of his neighbors called on him to congratulate him and to catch a glimpse of the hidden treasure. But the shrewd old farmer refused to let them have sight of it or tell them in which part of the house it was located.

Staten Island Folklore

BURIED TREASURE IN A VAULT

Destruction of Hatfield homestead at Port Richmond, Staten Island. reveals gold coin and bullion.

The old Hatfield homestead, which had stood on Richmond Avenue Port Richmond. Staten Island, since the Revolution, has been torn down.

Yesterday afternoon the chimney and foundation walls were razed by Melvin E. Wigant, of Port Richmond, who was under contract to remove the old material. Adjoining and partly under the foundation of the chimney in the cellar was found a vault made of old marble tombstones and slabs, I n which was found a quantity of gold coin and some bullion gold.

There were a number of witnesses of the finding of the gold, one was a Mr. John Redmond of New Brighton, who, when asked raised a handful of gold. Many a wild story speedily spread of the discovery of a great fortune. Mr. Wlgant, the proprietor of a livery stable, said last night that some gold had been found, but he said that the amount was not large.

Staten Island Folklore

The latest date found on any of the coins was 1866. Mr. Wigant. who Is an old Staten Islander and knew Jacob Hatfleld, who died some five years ago, said that he had always believed that Jacob or his father had money buried somewhere, but he had no Idea when he bought the old material that he would unearth it.

A tale of buried treasure on the Hatfield homestead circulated for years, probably because it was known that Jacob Hatfield was a bit eccentric, liberal enough to those he liked, but shrewd in business transactions.

There most assuredly was a legal battle for the treasure, because of all the stories about buried treasure, the owners of the property put in the bill of sale a special clause. In the bill of sale it stated . . . and it is further mutually agreed and covenanted that, the party of the first part, reserves to himself, and the party of the second part is to deliver to him, said party of the first part, any and all money, or moneys, jewels, gold, or silver, such findings to remain property of the party of the first part.

~ New York Tribune May 30, 1901 &
New York Times May 31, 1901

Staten Island Folklore

STATEN ISLAND'S HOUSE OF BURIED TREASURE
Located in Richmond Town

As it looks today

The Treasure House has stood at what is now the intersection of Richmond Road and Arthur Kill Road in Historic Richmond Town and has undergone incarnations as a tannery, a bakery, a shoe maker's shop and a post office.

Staten Island Folklore

From a 1921 story about the Treasure House . . . .

    It Recently Paid Its third fat dividend of eighteenth century gold, the second having been "declared" under the stairs in 1857.
    The house is at Richmondtown, Staten Island, built in 1752, which gives up buried treasure periodically.
    It is a ramshackle house, older by decades than the nation itself. It has fallen into some disrepair, but stands solidly nonetheless, for they built stoutly in those days. Its portals are guarded by a small cannon on a stone base and by a garish, red gasoline filling station, a blatant splash of modernity in the old-fashioned setting. The latter, considering the present quotations on automotive fuel, seems the more effective weapon of defense.
    Why the need for defense? You may ask.
    Because this is a treasure house. Not once, but thrice has it proved itself so. Three times, once recently, have buried troves been unearthed within and without its walls.
    But let this be a story of "Three Soldiers."

Staten Island Folklore

Let it be related by Colonel Homan, Major Hicks and Captain Connor, all good men.

Seated around a stove which functioned as if it, with the house, dated back to 1752 and rationed by a tower of ham sandwiches and a can of coffee, the three old Staten Islanders began to spin their yarn.

Flanked by ham sandwiches and a can of coffee, the three old Staten Islanders began to spin their yarn

Staten Island Folklore

"Well." Colonel Homan commenced by seniority of rank, right as householder, ownership of the treasure and sovereignty over any future finds, "I've been living in this house since 1867. Both as a man and and as a boy."

"That's a long time," said Captain Connor.
"It is that," agreed Major Hicks.

"Me now, I'm seventy-five years old," said the Colonel, with pardonable pride.

"Would you believe it?" demanded the Captain.

"No, you wouldn't." supplied the Major.

"Well, this house was built about a hundred years before I was born," the colonel continued. "And not so long after the house was built they started to fight the Revolution around here. The Americans had laid out and settled the town here"

"And right here," interposed Captain Connor "I have the first surveying' instrument ever used on Staten Island." He produced a queer old brass transit in a hand hewn wooden case." Can you beat that?"
"No, you can't," the Major assured.

"Well," the Colonel resumed, "the British came in here or rather they sent them Hessians in"

This had the town folk thinking, it was about time to hide away their money.

"I have a collection of that old paper money and coins," the Captain interrupted.

Staten Island Folklore

"Finest collection in the State of New York," the Major chimed in.

"So they started to bury all their treasures around these parts. There wasn't banks back then, you know. So folk sunk all their worldly possessions into the ground or hid it through their houses somewheres. Some dug under the roots of trees, thinking they'd have a fine landmark to find the stuff again. Then the trees blew down and when those folks or their children came back to look for the treasure they found the marks gone. Other ones kept the secrets, so you can't tell where you'll find treasure around these parts, and all kinds Captain Connor remarked,

"Over at my house I have got a collection of a lot of that old stuff. Right here's a copy of 'The Time Piece,' an old New York newspaper issued in 1798."

"He ought to charge admission to that collection" the Major declared admiringly.

Back in 1857 a man named Pat Hylan, who lived here, run across a treasure in that old stairway over there. A tin chuckful of British coins, $7,000 it was.

Staten Island Folklore

The old stairway where Pat Hylan found $7,000 in British sovereigns in the memorable year 1857.

The old stairway where Pat Hylan found $7,000 in British sovereigns in the memorable year 1857.

Staten Island Folklore

A bit later they found some more treasure out there where an old stone wall used to be.

"So I thought I oughta be finding a treasure myself", th Colonel stated.

The Colonel went on about the time that the Captain, who was leasing this property from him, started digging and putting down a gasoline tank out front of the house. A smiling Colonel reminded the Captain of the stipulation he had put in the lease. That was if any treasure be found while digging on his property, that treasure would be his.

The Captain chimed in, don't you suppose there is more treasure around this old house.

The Colonels last remarks were "I'll say this: If this house is ever torn down, I'm going to be here day and night'

~ New York Tribune October 30, 1921

Staten Island Folklore

Staten Island Folklore

Folklore

Staten Island Folklore

The Cost of Guilt

Richmond County Court House and Jail, Richmond, Staten Island, N.Y.

This is the common story of a neighbors' quarrel over land and property which results in a law suit, mutual recrimination, hate and revenge.

Staten Island Folklore

There is finally an accidental meeting of the parties and one of them kills the other. The scene is laid in a typical American county and the trial which takes place in a typical country village collects the people from every part of the vicinity, the little Court House is too small, and the court adjourns to the church which will hold more people, but which is crowded to the doors. The killing is admitted, but fortunately the prisoner has a better reputation among his neighbors, who are trying him, than has his victim. The solemnity of the place, the awful occasion on which the auditory had assembled, the situation of the prisoner and his weeping relatives who are all present, combine to excite a peculiar sympathy in his favor, which is heightened by the eloquent appeal to the jury made by his counsel. The jury after seven hours' deliberation returned a verdict of not guilty, and the prisoner went free but not before receiving from the judge a caution which he probably never forgot for a single instant as long as he lived.

In October 1815, Bornt Lake, residing on the Amboy Road, a few rods south of the Black Horse Tavern, while returning from his father's house, was shot and killed on the public road in front of his own premises, by his next door neighbor, Christian Smith.

Immediately after the commission of the deed, Smith went to another neighbor, John Jackson, and informed him of what he had done, and asked his advice as to what he should do. What advice his neighbor gave him is not known. Smith wandered about the woods, where he was found later in the day, and taken to prison. He did not deny having committed the murder, but justified himself by the plea that " Lake was committing a trespass upon his property; that he had frequently done the same thing, and had been warned repeatedly what the consequence would be if he did not desist."

The prosecution had an easy task, for the crime was not, and could not be denied; but the defense was justification. It was proved that a feud had for a long time existed between the parties, and that they did what they could to aggravate and annoy each other. Judge Spencer charged strongly against the prisoner, in accordance with the law. " If," said he, " the murdered man had trespassed upon the property of the prisoner, the law afforded ample redress, and he had no right to take the law in his own hand and redress his own wrongs."

The jury, however, took a different view of the

matter. They acquitted the prisoner. The people from everywhere were surprised at the result, and perhaps none more so than the prisoner himself.

Smith killed Bornt Lake because the latter insisted on crossing Smith's land. There was no doubt of his guilt, but he was acquitted for the very good reason, as given by one of the jurors, that, "if we convict the prisoner the judge will give him two or three months more to live, during which time the county will be obliged to feed him and to keep his cell warm, which would cost a good deal of money. If to this is added the cost of building a gallows, the sheriff's fee for hanging him, the cost of burying him, the expenses will amount to a hundred or a hundred and fifty dollars, and all of which will have to be raised by taxation ; but if on the other hand we say 'not guilty' every dollar of this amount will be saved."

Judge Spencer was indignant, and in discharging the prisoner from custody, was bitterly severe when he said "Christian Smith, you have been tried and acquitted by a jury of your country, for having taken away the life of one of your fellow creatures. I mean not to censure the jury who acquitted you, it is not my province so to do; I hope they will be able, upon future consideration, to reconcile their verdict to their consciences. But I should feel myself wanting in my duty as a man, if I did not express my opinion that, notwithstanding their verdict, I consider you a guilty, a very guilty man. Upon an ancient grudge, you considered yourself justified in doing what you have done; and the jury have, I fear, confirmed your false and fatal judgment. But, beware, you have not yet escaped. Believe me, your most awful trial is yet to come. You are now an old man, and your days may be few in this world, and you will shortly be compelled to appear before another court, where there is no jury but God himself. Unless you repent, and devote your future life to an humble atonement of your guilt, your condemnation there is certain. I am thus plain with you, in order that those who have listened to your trial, may learn that whatever may be considered to be the law of Staten Island, your conduct is unjustifiable in the sight of God and man"

Staten Island Folklore

Staten Island Folklore

The Wrath of a Young Damsel

The island played a significant role in the American Revolutionary War. On March 17, 1776, the British forces under Lord William Howe evacuated Boston and sailed for Halifax, Nova Scotia. From Halifax, Howe prepared to attack New York City, which then consisted entirely of

Staten Island Folklore

the southern end of Manhattan Island. General George Washington led the entire Continental Army to New York City in anticipation of the British attack. Howe used the strategic location of Staten Island as a staging ground for the invasion. Over 140 British ships arrived over the summer of 1776 and anchored off the shores of Staten Island at the entrance to New York Harbor, which was the largest armada to set sail until the Second World War. The British troops and Hessian mercenaries numbered at about 30,000. Howe established his headquarters in New Dorp at the Rose and Crown Tavern near the junction of present New Dorp Lane and Amboy Road.

The maids of Staten Island wrought havoc among the royal troops who were quartered among them during the Revolution. Near quarantine, in an old house, the Austen mansion, a soldier of King George hanged himself because a Yankee maid who lived there would not have him for a husband, nor any gentleman whose coat was of his color; and, until ghosts went out of fashion, his spirit, in somewhat heavy boots, with jingling spurs, often disturbed the nightly quiet of the place.

The conduct of a damsel in the old town of

Staten Island Folklore

Richmond was even more stern. She was the granddaughter, and a pretty one, of a farmer named Britton; but though Britton by descent and name, she was no friend of Britons, albeit she might have had half the officers in the neighboring camp at her feet, if she had wished them there. Once, while mulling a cup of cider for her grandfather, she was interrupted by a self-invited myrmidon, who undertook, in a fashion rude and unexpected, to show the love in which he held her. Before he could kiss her, the girl drew the hot poker from the mug of drink and jabbed at the vitals of her amorous foe, burning a hole through his scarlet uniform and printing on his burly person a lasting memento of the adventure. With a howl of pain the fellow rushed away, and the privacy of the Britton family was never again invaded, at least whilst cider was being mulled.

Staten Island Folklore

Staten Island Folklore

The Indian Lady

Shooters Island

There is a legend of an eccentric lady from Shooters Island who used to be seen walking the Terrace between Mariners Harbor and Port

Staten Island Folklore

Richmond. This area had beautiful homes in an area called Captains Row. For decades, one could see, on any given day, the travels of a woman who came to be known as "The Indian Lady" Her world consisted of those few short miles of the terrace carrying all her worldly possessions. It has been told that she carried everything in cardboard boxes tied with brightly colored string. She dressed as if it was winter even in the deep heat of summer. She wore a long trench coat and always had a hat on. Common lore has it that in summertime she lived on Shooters Island and would row her boat over to the terrace to get supplies, when weather got rough in the winter she lived across from St. Mary of the Assumption 2230 Richmond Terrace, in a building near the water owned by the Salazo brothers (Salazos' owned the property before Edkins junk yard, they were Forest Oil) The house belonged to them as told by John Salazo. People remember seeing her on the 'Avenue' – that is Richmond Avenue in Port Richmond around 1956-1958. Some have said that she lived well over 100 years old and that she died in the old farm colony. According to legend, she never spoke to anyone, just went on about her business. She had very long hair and wore long

Staten Island Folklore

old fashioned clothing – with her coat held closed with safety pins.

She used to bring her boat into many different places in Mariner's Harbor, Surkos Lumber, Brewers Shipyard and any other place that would let her tie up. She would than catch the bus and go to Manhattan. Turns out to be, there was a reason she went to Manhattan – more about that later.

A friend of mine related this story to me . . . .

In the fifties I lived at 2180 Richmond Terrace opposite Faber Pool, my parents were the custodians of the Knights of Columbus hall at that location, and we occupied the apartment above it. The Indian Lady would pass by, several times a week, she pulled her boat in by the junkyard and would walk from there to Richmond Avenue to pick up provisions. She may have dressed loudly, but I never heard anybody bothering her, nor she bothering them.

During the summer, she lived on Shooters Island in an old shack, but if the winter was cold, the owner of the scrap metal shop, opposite St. Marys Church (St. Mary of the Assumption 2230 Richmond Terrace) let her live in an apartment there. She may have been an eccentric, but she always held her head up, and gave the neighborhood some flair, and all the old maids something to talk about.

    This is from a visitor to my website – in response to your inquiry about the Indian Lady, I grew up around 1952 on Sharpe Avenue and used to swim in the river at the foot of Sharpe Avenue. I was 8 years old, well, she lived right there on the waterfront in 1952 and even then she was haggard. I would guess she had a very hard life. She was about 40 to 45 years old, of course now that doesn't seem elderly ... but back then..... wow.. .. I never heard anyone mention her from shooters Island..   I really don't know much about her as she was always a recluse, as a kid I said hello to her but only once cause she sorta HISSSSed at me and that was the end of my hellos... she wore a ton of old clothes and they always were dirty , she chopped wood in her yard for heat and I suspect to cook on ...her hands and face always seemed "sooty"

    In the early years, I recall she always had 2 or 3 shopping bags with her, of course we kids always thought they were full of money. Years later she always pushed or dragged a shopping cart, the type with 2 wheels. I think she passed on in the late 70s or maybe the early 80s, I do know I read her obituary in the S.I. Advance and

Staten Island Folklore

they mentioned her as being known as the Indian Lady. I don't know for sure but I seem to remember something about them finding a large sum of money, but on the other hand that could be a fantasy in my head. To sum it all up, I suspect she was just an old woman with no family who somehow found herself in a lousy situation... oh... the nickname Indian Lady was, I suspect because she used to wear lots of dresses (yes ,all at the same time) that were kind of bright and about mid calf... like you would see in a picture of an Indian girl .. she didn't look "ethnically" like an Indian..... just an old lady.

Another persons memories of her . . . .

Of the Indian Lady she says: " As always on her regular and much repeated way, back and forth, for decades, between Port Richmond and Mariners Harbor, the Indian Lady carried all of her worldly goods in cardboard boxes tied with string. She wore floor length topcoats and scarves over her hair and a fedora in any weather. She had long thick black hair and according to my mother had been, in her day, a great beauty.

All these bits and pieces led me to do further research, here is some of what I uncovered . . . .

I learned that the Indian Lady had come to settle on Shooters Island looking for a quiet and placid place and to escape the literary colony of Greenwich Village. She was a writer of books, a vegetarian and a gymnast. She was known to have grown tired of the hotels in Manhattan. The Indian Lady came to be known by the name India Mount Clemon, this is the name the boatmen of the Terrace used for her. One of the boatmen had said of her, "Some think she was a princess. She has been all over the world and she knows everything"

This may seem like the story of a homeless, bag lady, but as I have learned, the Indian Lady was far more then that. Eccentric may be a good word to describe her.

The Indian Lady lived on a yacht off of Shooters Island, the yacht was 90 feet long and valued at $90,000 when new. She obtain it from a boating firm in Manhattan for very little money, since it required many expensive repairs. She would hire the boatmen from the Terrace to help with the repairs on the yacht. While on Shooters Island she never mingled with the 20 or so people who also resided on the Island. It is told that she only talked to people when she needed work done, then she was very courteous and said to be a generous tipper.

India was a health enthusiast who did not like

extremes in temperature. If the temperature dropped too much while she was on Shooters Island, she would head to Manhattan where she had a suite at the famous Wolcott Hotel. This hotel was located on 31st Street and Fifth Avenue. Many famous people have stayed at this hotel, including Buddy Holly and famed author Edith Wharton.

Staten Island Folklore

Shooters Island as it was in 1924

A Little About Shooters Island . . .

The island was essentially made by infill from early dredging of Newark Bay in the 19th century

Staten Island Folklore

Shooters Island is a 43-acre uninhabited island at the southern end of Newark Bay, along the north shore of Staten Island. The boundary between the states of New York and New Jersey runs through the island, with a small portion on the north end of the island belonging to the cities of Bayonne and Elizabeth in New Jersey and the rest being part of the borough of Staten Island in New York City.

In colonial times Shooter's Island was used as a hunting preserve. During the Revolutionary War, George Washington used the island as a drop-off point for messages, and the place became a haven for spies.

From approximately 1900 until 1910 it was a major shipyard, the Townsend-Downey Shipbuilding, Company. The entire island was occupied by buildings, foundry , pattern shop, offices, etc. There were major docks and ship ways which faced to the east. Contrary to a previous report, President Theodore Roosevelt did not go hunting on this industrial island but rather the Townsend-Downey Company built a yacht, The Meteor III for the Kaiser Wilhelm of Germany. It was launched at Shooters Island in February 1902 and was accompanied by many hundreds of spectators.

Staten Island Folklore

Thomas Alva Edison sent a camera man over and made one of the first news movies in US history of the event. It is available online from the Smithsonian. Alice Roosevelt christened the boat and father Teddy was there as well. The following day a reception was held at the White House for Mr. Downey and representatives of the German Government.

The following year saw the launching of one of the fastest and most famous sailing vessels in history, the 3 masted Schooner Atlantic. In 1905 it raced across the Atlantic and won the Kaiser's cup and set the record for the crossing under sail, which stood unbroken for almost 90 years. Another famous vessel built on Shooters Island was the Carnegie, named after Andrew Carnegie who was a friend of Mr. Downey. It was built for scientific research and constructed of wood with no iron or steel that would cause magnetic anomalies. All fastenings and metal parts were of non magnetic bronze.

Unmaintained during much of the later 20th century, the island has been made an official bird sanctuary, partially to discourage the United States Army Corps of Engineers who wanted to blow up the island to ease navigation by vessels coming down from Port Newark. It has begun to disintegrate into Newark Bay. The island and decayed remnants of old piers are visible to users of the Bayonne Bridge between Staten Island and Bayonne, New Jersey. The remains of the once active shipyard are still present, but diminishing every year.

Shooter's Island began to support nesting wading birds, cormorants and gulls in the early 1970s. At its peak in 1995, the island supported 400 nesting pairs of herons, egrets, ibis and 121 nesting pairs of double-crested cormorants. The island is now owned by the City of New York and is maintained by New York City Department of Parks and Recreation as a bird sanctuary.

Staten Island Folklore

Staten Island Folklore

Ichabod Crane

Staten Island Folklore

Ichabod Crane, the schoolteacher who met the Headless Horseman was a fictional character in Washington Irving's short story The Legend of Sleepy Hollow, first published in 1820. Irving may have borrowed the name from that of a colonel in the US Army during the War of 1812 whom he had once met, also named Ichabod Crane.

Colonel Ichabod Crane actually service in two branches of the military. From 1809 to 1812 he served in the United States Marines, then from 1812 on he served in the United States Army.

In 1853, Crane and his wife Charlotte (May 25, 1798 – September 25, 1878) bought an old farmhouse, in Travis and shortly after had the structure greatly enlarged and remodeled had a house built in the New Springville – Travis section of Staten Island in 1853, He was still on active duty during this time. The house was located at 3525 Victory Blvd; it was demolished in March of 1989. The owner had offered it to Historic Richmond Town, on the condition they move it off its former site; it never transpired due to a lack of funding.

Crane died in Port Richmond in October of 1857 while still on active duty, and is buried in Asbury Methodist Cemetery, in New Springville, not far from his former home.

Soldiers who served under Colonel Crane's command erected the seven-foot marble monument to him at Asbury Cemetery after his death in 1857. His grave marker bears the inscription:

"He served his country faithfully for 48 years and was much beloved and respected by all who knew him"

The Ichabod Crane House, pictured on the next page, was originally built in the early nineteenth century by Ozais Ansley as a small one and a half story farmhouse. Colonel Crane, a career officer in the United States Army, bought this farmhouse and the surrounding five acres in 1854

Staten Island Folklore

SACRED TO THE MEMORY OF
COL. ICHABOD B. CRANE
OF THE U.S. ARMY
WHO WAS BORN IN
ELIZABETH TOWN N.J.
JULY 18, 1787
DIED ON STATEN ISLAND
OCTOBER 5.TH 1857
HE SERVED HIS
COUNTRY FAITHFULLY
48 YEARS AND WAS MUCH
BELOVED AND RESPECTED
BY ALL WHO KNEW HIM

Staten Island Folklore

Ichabod Crane Monument Asbury Methodist Cemetery

Staten Island Folklore

Staten Island Folklore

Staten Island Folklore

Lady in Blue

The photos were taken close to the time of the incident but not by me. It's weird but TRUE! Here is the story of The Lady in Blue. I was born and raised in Pleasant Plains on Staten Island, NYC.

In the mid 1960's when I was around 15, I, like all the other kids in NYC neighborhoods, hung out downtown in front of the corner Drug Store.

Staten Island Folklore

One afternoon one of the girls who lived a few towns away needed to leave for home so I offered to walk her to the train station.

Both sides of the train station in our town were elevated. About 20 feet above street level. Both only had one way up and down and no way to get from one side to the other without going down to the street and crossing under the trestle and back up the other side. Otherwise it was a long drop if you tried to jump. The south bound side had 3 or 4 flights of stairs leading to the platform with only a small overhang for shelter. The north bound side (first photo is looking north on northbound side) had about the same number of stairs but went straight up to the platform (to where the lady is standing in the photo). On the northbound side was also a building (see photo) that had the old ticket counter and waiting area. You could still get inside for shelter but it wasn't used for much else at the time.

As we walked down the sidewalk toward the station we had to pass the south bound stairs go under the trestle and up the north bound stairs to get to the north bound train. As we approached the south bound side, sitting on the bottom step was a very old woman wearing a nice blue dress with big wide brimmed blue hat. As we got closer we could see that she was not pale completed but white with bright red lips. As kids we laughed to ourselves and commented on how bad this old woman looked with all that white make up. It would be the last time we would laugh that day.

We passed by within a few feet of her and she looked as real as anyone, just a bit stranger looking. She seemed pleasant however and smiled a big smile at us as we passed. We then walked the next 100 or so feet, went under the trestle and turned to walk up the stairs to the North bound side. We took the first step, then looked up to the top and there was the old lady looking down at us smiling (she was standing about where the lady in the photo is). We quickly looked at each other in amazement and then back, but she wasn't there anymore.

We continued climbing to the top of the stairs which were at the northern most end of the platform. When we reached the top the lady was not on the station platform. We walked half way down the platform (where the man in this second photo is) and into the waiting area but she wasn't there either. So we came back out.

Sort of half laughing about the whole thing when we noticed the lady was standing at the top of the stairs where we just walked up and where we first saw her. But we didn't pass her? We stepped back inside for a brief moment to get hold of ourselves and when we came out again she was at the far opposite end of the platform with her back to us looking in the direction of where the train would come from (we were standing about where the man is. Looking toward the far end in the photo). We went to the right and to the opposite side of the platform (where the woman in the photo is) from her to wait for the train as the girl wanted to get on the first car. We stopped and turned around and the lady was no longer there. Now we were concerned that maybe she had fallen off the platform or that we were totally crazy. Maybe we just missed seeing her all those times. But, we hadn't turned our backs on her long enough for her to get to the waiting room and now the train was in view coming into the station. We could see the whole platform and it was empty except for us.

    I told the girl I would go check to see where the old lady went after she got on the train. We stood looking in the direction of the incoming train with the full station in view. The train pulled in and stopped. The girl got on the first car (I was standing about where the woman in the photo is standing) and I went up to her window and knocked on it to say goodbye. I waved goodbye as the train pulled out of the station only to have my blood run cold when I noticed the lady in Blue sitting behind the girl smiling at me as the train pulled away.

    I ran home and kept calling the girl until she got home and answered the phone. I told her what I saw and she said that when she paid the conductor she changed her seat and there was

Staten Island Folklore

no one else there in the car.

    Now, not many people believe this story but we both experienced it. I never saw the girl again and never told the story until I was in my thirties. Since then I have heard of a few other people having a sighting there of the lady in blue.

    ~ Kim Kowalczyk   www.ghostbreakers.com

Staten Island Folklore

Staten Island Folklore

Staten Island Folklore

Palace Theater

Staten Island Folklore

Headline . . . .
The estate of woman put near a million dollars.

    A 90 year old widow, Mrs. Emma Buhl de Hart died on May 28, 1957. She lived in a modest apartment at 104 Port Richmond Avenue. Mrs. De Hart was, according to her neighbors, a fragile little lady, who owned a two story building in which she lived frugally and alone on the top floor. She owned the building right next to hers which was the famous Palace Theater. Her attorneys stated that Mrs. Emma de Hart owned many, many acres of undeveloped land near the Proctor & Gamble soap company plant at Port Ivory.
    Neighbors, concerned that they did not see Emma for a few days, called the police. A niece of hers was called and the police knocked down the door and found a very sick Mrs. Hart. An ambulance had transported her to Sunnyside Hospital where she passed away. Her death was attributed to a kidney ailment and heart condition, complicated by malnutrition. She was buried in Fairview Cemetery on Victory Blvd. Her husband, Samuel De Hart was a tugboat owner and he

died eleven years before his wife.

Family petitioned the court for a search warrant to look for her will in the apartment. Only two of the six room were found to be livable. Four rooms were filled with old newspapers, magazines and letters. Fire had damaged the apartment years ago but no repairs were ever made. She lived with no telephone and only a pot bellied stove for heat. The stove was used in place of her gas and electric heaters so she could save money. Old crates and newspapers were burned in the pot bellied stove. Though she looked to be a well bred and dignified woman, she would haggle over prices of groceries at the local stores. Neighbors, talking about Mrs. Hart, spoke of her daily routine. She would walk the neighborhood about noon each day, walk to a local 5&10 and have either a hot dog or hamburger for lunch. If weather permitted she would sit in a chair outside her home. Then she would go up to her apartment, listen to a radio and retire about 7:30 PM each night. Mrs. Emma De Hart had built, owned and then sold the Palace Movie Theater on Richmond Avenue and then had sold it. According to family members, Mrs De Hart was responsible for building up Richmond Avenue into a bustling shopping district.

Staten Island Folklore

There was never a will to be found in the search of the apartment, but what was found, under a bed, in three cardboard boxes was a fortune. $274,980 in cash was found. The bills were in denominations from tens to thousand dollar bills. The hundred dollars bills alone totaled $220,100. In addition to the cash, bank books were found with an amount of $205,000 and 740 shares of securities were discovered. The common stock was of International Nickel, Standard Oil and Woolworths.

Mrs. De Harts husband was a member of an old Staten Island family. He was related to May and Viola De Hart, elderly twin sisters who were recluses. They were clubbed to death in their Staten Island home in 1946 by a distant cousin, Gorden De Hart, in the theft of $500. He served nine years in prison for manslaughter.

Staten Island Folklore

Staten Island Folklore

Staten Island Folklore

Nazi War Prisoner

Staten Island Folklore

Emanuel Kalytka

In June of 1944, the army's Halloran General Hospital (this became Willowbrook State School) was the sight of a huge manhunt. A 29 year old German prisoner of war had escaped from this hospital and was the object of a massive manhunt. The New York Metropolitan area had never seen the likes of such an intensive manhunt.

Staten Island Folklore

Halloran General Hospital

Troops, armed with machine guns were stationed at the three bridges and five ferry docks that connected Staten Island to the mainland. At bridges police were stopping and searching all automobiles. The Coast Guard were patrolling the waters around the Island for any sign of the escapee.

Posses of Staten Island residents formed to search the Island after news of the prisoner escapee had circulated. Even baseball games across the Island were stopped and the players, armed with bats, took joined in the search. Bloodhounds were brought down from upstate to help in the search. As night fell you could see, all across the Island, search lights from the army vehicles that had descended on Staten Island.

The search for this escaped prisoner was so big it included the Army, the Coast Guard, the police, and the FBI. An alarm about this escape had been sent to nines states. All vehicles leaving the island were searched. The FBI had described the Nazi prisoner as age - 29, height - 5 feet 9 inches, weight – 165 pounds, complexion – fair and sunburned. They also reported that he spoke broken English but was fluent in both German and Polish.

The 29 year old Kalytka had a plan. He had been in the hospital just a short time and he made it a practice to stay in bed all day on Sundays, not even going down for meals. This routine must have been his plan to get a head start before his escape was even noticed. So, before 7AM on this Sunday morning the Nazi prisoner calmly slipped out of a second story barracks window. And somehow slipped passed all the mounted police that surround the area.

Two days after the escape the FBI announced that the search had ended. At 1:45 PM on June 13, 1944 the Staten Island police department was asked by the hospital to give up the search. A short time later a hospital spokesman issued this statement "The prisoner has been captured". Captured? Not really, more like, he gave up. Tired and hungry the escapee returned.

It wasn't easy for the prisoner to hide since he was clothed in a green prisoner's uniform with P.W. Painted in white on the back of the coat and the seat of the trousers. After avoiding capture by military, police and civilian search parties,

Staten Island Folklore

Emanuel Kalytka returned to the hospital, from which he escaped from just in time for lunch. An officer from the hospital quoted Kalytka as saying "I just wanted to see the good old United States". After a stroll through Clove Lakes Park the prisoner said he spent must of Sunday sleeping. Before dawn on Monday he found his way to a heavily wooded area of Sea View Hospital where he slept in the brush. Monday night he could hear searchers in the woods looking for him. The Major from the hospital said of Kalytka, he was tired and hungry and just wanted to get back to the hospital for some good food. Tuesday, before dawn, he managed to reenter the hospital as easily as he had left it two days earlier, past the guards and stay in the basement area until the noon meal was served. There he slipped into the line of prisoners marching to the mess hall and was in the midst of the meal when he was discovered. He was apprehended in the mess hall, eating lunch. Uncle Sam, under international code, feeds prisoners according to the standards of feeding for his own fighting men under similar conditions. The meal consisted of cream of mushroom soup, roast veal, potatoes, carrots, lettuce salad, chocolate cake and milk. It is told that the prisoner was interrupted during the first course but, after questioning was returned to finish his meal.

The FBI's secret was out, because people in this area had no idea that prisoners of war were being housed in their own backyards. This lead to the discovery that German and Italian prisoners were being used as general laborers in the army hospital situated on the 383-acre Willowbrook Park estate.

Probable to save face, the FBI had announced in the June 13th, 1944 edition of the New York Post that the prisoner was recaptured in the New Dorp section.

The hospital was generally used to treat wounded American soldiers. In 1945 it was learned that there was upwards of 145 German prisoners at Halloran Hospital.

Staten Island Folklore

Staten Island Folklore

Staten Island Folklore

Queen Elizabeth II

Staten Island Folklore

October 21, 1957

The Queen had asked to be brought into New York City through Staten Island. Here reasoning was that Manhattan should be approached by sea, so that she may see the famous skyline. In her words "It is a sight I have seen many times in pictures and this time I would love to see it in person" Queen Elizabeth II and Prince Philip travel on a special train from a meeting with President Dwight D. Eisenhower in Washington, D.C., along the former North Shore rail tracks. The Queens party crossed the Arthur Kill on a twelve car B&O Railroad from Washington DC, they traveled along the defunct North Shore Rail line and departed at a freight station in Stapleton. The Queen descended onto a sixty-five foot red carpet. There the Queen and Prince Philip were greeted at by then Governor Harriman. Just a few minutes later a motorcade started a mile and a half trip to St. George. They then sailed aboard an Army ferryboat named Lieutenant Samuel S Coursen across New York Harbor passing the Statue of Liberty.

Staten Island Folklore

July 9, 1976

Queen Elizabeth II visits Manhattan during the 1976 Bicentennial festivities. Her journey through the Upper Bay on July 9, 1976 delayed Staten Island Ferry service for 90 minutes. She departed from the slip 6 at the St. George ferry terminal with her husband, prince Phillip, after a motorcade along Bay St. which was lined with 23,000 islanders pressing against police barricades to catch sight of the queen on her initial visit to the United States. Service on the Staten Island Ferry was interrupted for almost an hour and a half today Britain's Queen Elizabeth II cruised from the U.S. Army Military Ocean Terminal in Bayonne to the Battery in Manhattan amid elaborate security precautions.

Staten Island Folklore

Staten Island Folklore

The Lindbergh Baby

Staten Island Folklore

Did someone on Staten Island have something to do with the kidnapping of the Lindbergh's baby? Some of the newspaper headlines of the day say maybe it was so.

CHECK NEW REPORT OF BABY IN COUPE; Police Hear Car Like Johnson's Crossed From Perth Amboy to Tottenville Tuesday Night. LICENSE NUMBER SIMILAR Toll Collector Belatedly Reveals Three Adults and Child Were Headed for New York. March 9, 1932, Wednesday A possibility that the kidnappers of the Lindbergh baby crossed in a green coupe from Perth Amboy, N.J., to Tottenville, S.I., at about 10:45 P.M. on the night the baby was stolen from his crib at Hopewell, N.J., was revealed yesterday by information filed with the Port Authority.

VETERAN AGAIN HELD IN NEW RANSOM PLOT; Man Convicted in Lindbergh Case Now Accused of Threats to Staten Island Woman.

EX-SOLDIER QUERIED IN LINDBERGH CASE; Staten Island Man Is Taken to New Jersey on Clue Given in an Unsigned Letter. Cooperates

Staten Island Folklore

with police Mulrooney. Denies inquiry is Linked With offer of "information" on kidnapping of child. December 28, 1932, Wednesday On information contained in an unsigned letter received by the Newark police, detectives from that city and New York questioned Hollister Demo of 52 Van Pelt Avenue, Mariners Harbor, Staten Island, yesterday afternoon and evening as to his movements on the night of March 1, when the Lindbergh baby was kidnapped at Hopewell, N.J. August 2, 1934 Golford Clobridge, 34 years old, a disabled war veteran, who was arrested in Miami in 1933 for sending a $50,000 ransom note to Colonel Charles A. Lindbergh after the kidnapping of the Lindbergh baby, was arrested again on Staten Island yesterday.

Staten Island Folklore

Staten Island Folklore

Indian Caves

Housman's Cave

In the sloping hillside facing Richmond Turnpike near the junction of Little Clove Road is Staten Island's only remaining cave. The hill, some thirty or forty years ago, was beautifully wooded with large beech and oak trees and the finest grove of white pines on the island. A thick growth of underbrush screened the entrance to the cave and it could not be seen until the searcher had made his way through the protecting screen and was in its immediate vicinity. Most of the trees have died during recent years or have been cut down, and fires have destroyed nearly all of the underbrush; but even now the entrance is not conspicuous and would be likely to escape the attention of any casual observer a short distance away.

It has been a matter of surprise to me to learn that so many of our residents are apparently unaware of its existence, and as it is almost certain to be destroyed before very long I have thought it advisable that the attention of our members should be called to it and an illustrated record be prepared for our Proceedings.

At the meeting of the Association on October 10, 1903, Mr. William T. Davis read a paper on Staten Island Caves, in which he says "this cave is not a natural one; but according to local history it and some other holes in the hillside were dug, shortly after the Revolution, by Housman and his Negro servant in their search for gold." What Housman's

given name may have been I have not been able to find any record. Clute, in his Annals of Staten Island (p. 121), refers to him as "a young man named Housman [who] resided in the vicinity of the Four Corners," and says (p. 122): "This same Housman, in after years, conceived the idea that there was great mineral wealth in the hills about the Four Corners, and with the aid of a Negro commenced mining operations in the side of the hill, in what is called Dongan's wood"... the excavation which he made in the solid rock . . . may be seen at the present day." Anthon's notes likewise contain merely a very vague reference. Mr. Hine's memorandum is as follows: " All Anthon says is ' on the property lately belonging to Walter Dongan is a cave. The grandfather of the present Housman dug it to get gold after a dream.That is all he has to say. At another point he speaks of talking with Isaac Housman who. I think, was living in the Black Horse Tavern at the time (1853"). This may be ' the present Housman'; but this is a mere guess." That is all that I have been able to ascertain in regard to the origin of the cave.
~ proceedings of the Staten Island Association of Arts and Sciences - 1916

Staten Island Folklore

From the skating ring you walk up the path that runs sort of parallel to Victory Blvd. There's another entrance to that path that comes from the side walk, just keep going parallel to Victory Blvd. about half way to the top and go left up the hill in the woods. It's somewhere on that hill. There are rocks all around it and you can tell it was once a cave.
The following conclusion about the Clove Lake Caves is from Dorothy Valentine Smith's book, Staten Island – Gateway to New York. "There's even a place further up the hill among the sassafras and elder bushes that small boys solemnly swear was an Indian cave. Indians are far more exciting to talk about than how the shaft really got there - through the excavating efforts of a man named Houseman who, soon after the Revolution, was hunting for gold in the serpentine rock.".

Staten Island Folklore

Staten Island Folklore

Staten Island Folklore

German Submarine

Staten Island Folklore

Not sure if it was the Can-Can sale or what but there is a story being told throughout the years of a submarine off the Staten Island shore. It has been heard from many sources, including folks in the Coast Guard and Ferry Boat Captains. Apparently, during World War II a German submarine was able to sneak by the patrols at Sandy Hook and enter lower New York Harbor and Raritan Bay.

Although one would think that the New York Harbor was always safe from a foreign military invasion, there have been times in recent history when enemy forces operated just outside of the harbor. In World War 2, the Battle of the Atlantic came to the shores of America.

A steel net was sunk across the Verrazano Narrows between Brooklyn and Staten Island to keep German submarines out of the inner harbor. German submarines did plant mines around Sandy Hook, and 16 tug boats based at Staten Island were turned into minesweepers. "Working in pairs, they swept the ocean every day for 100 miles out from Sandy Hook, finding and exploding a large number of floating mines".

Two vessels were stationed at the nets and had no propulsion of their own, so they were moved by tugs. Each had a power generator for

Staten Island Folklore

electricity and steam. One of the was equipped with hydrophones for underwater listening, and one magneto telephone to Hoffman Island. This was connected to the Harbor Entrance Command Post at Fort Wadsworth and to Swinburne Island, the site of the Degaussing Section (Degaussing is the process of decreasing or eliminating an unwanted magnetic field). This vessel was also equipped with one 50 caliber and two 30 caliber machine guns. The other vessel was equipped only with visual signaling equipment and armed with Thompson machine guns.

After crossing the Atlantic Ocean, the German U-boats began their assault on American shipping on Jan 12, 1942, when Captain Hardegan and his crew of the U-123 sunk the "Cyclops" off Nova Scotia, and the war entered New York waters on Jan 14, 1942, when the U-123 sunk the "Norness" 60 miles off Montauk Point, Long Island.

On the next evening, the U-123 was following a parallel course westward along the south shore of Long Island, towards New York City. The submarine almost itself beached on the Rockaway shore, as the crew did not have detailed charts of the area and did not anticipate the southward curve of the Rockaways. From the reports of the area including the description of " a hotel, shore lights, and sand dunes backed by low, dark woods" (possibly Staten Island).

When a loop or hydrophone detected a possible enemy submarine in the harbor, a submarine net located at the Narrows between Fort Wadsworth in Staten Island and Fort Hamilton in Brooklyn was closed. A net tender vessel was stationed at this normally open net, and closed the net upon orders from the Harbor Entrance Control Post.

As our story goes the submarine had broached the surface near Huguenot and launched a rubber life boat. The crew came ashore, went to town, bought or stole groceries and returned to the ship undetected.

From a news source . . . .

In September of 1939 submarines were seen off the New Jersey Coast. Off the shores of Atlantic City, New Jersey four boat crews reported the citing of submarines along the coast but none of the four were able to determine if they were foreign ships.

The Captain of a buoy tender was near Staten Island when he spotted four submarines making there way down the coast.

A gentleman on his yacht twenty miles off Barnegat Light (near Toms River, NJ) was fishing

Staten Island Folklore

when he eyed a submarine in the waters.

A report of a submarine citing came from a yacht twenty five miles southeast off Atlantic City, NJ shore.

A submarine hastily arose then submerged about forty miles off Delaware Bay at 2 o'clock, according to crew members of the tanker Japan Arrow. The tanker is owned by the Socony Vacuum Oil Company and they reported this to the Radio Marine Corporation. A brief report was also given to the Coast Guard Air Base at Cape May, NJ.

The Coast Guard stated that no planes were sent to the area because they had received no special instruction from the Treasure Department or the coast guard Headquarters.

There was a cutter name Mohawk that was patrolling the area in which the submarine was reported . Also there has been increased vigilance on behalf of seven small cutter craft assigned to this district.

As a side note to this story. . . a few months before I had finished this book and was getting it ready for publication, I got an interesting email from an old timer from Midland Beach. It was about a submarine and I just had to add it to this tale.

Staten Island Folklore

This is the email word for word. . .
Midland Beach ...was a beautiful amusement area..with a merry go round and a bank-- a winery....many - many buildings.... on the beach...they used to set up a big screen - and show movies...
One night ...I was about five years old I guess...there was a lot of "buzz" from the people there. There were POW's ...that helped clean the beach ..and one of them said that there was a SUBMARINE watching the movie with their "BIG EYES"...the big periscope on deck....
INDEED -- there was a SUB out there...and several Germans actually came ashore and bought ice cream and other things - and went back to the sub by rowboat...
This was close to the end of the war... When the war ended - the sub surrendered in MASS...and the Boston PD got all the weapons from her

Staten Island Folklore

Staten Island Folklore

Staten Island Folklore

The Eccentric Mr. Organ

Ec·cen·tric adj   \ik-'sen-trik,

Definition of Eccentric
: deviating from an established or usual pattern or style
: deviating from conventional or accepted usage or conduct especially in odd or whimsical ways

    This mans name came up many times from visitors to my website. Here is a story from some emails I received about him. He sounded like a real character, though by todays standards, I believe parents would be a bit leary of him.
    In 1947 Mr. Organ came into my life through an introduction by a childhood friend, Gordon W. Gordon and I attended Sunday school together and he was about the only friend I had outside of school (of whom Nana approved) before the age of nine. Gordon was also responsible for my joining the Cub Scouts so, although he died ignominiously at age sixteen, he was a terrific influence in my life.

Staten Island Folklore

I believe I was ten-years-old when Gordon petitioned Mr. Organ to allow me into his private "club." The only new members admitted were those petitioned by current members. How, and why, he started his private "club" is another of life's mysteries I wish I'd had the perspicacity to explore in 1947, but who has that kind of understanding at eleven? Not I.

Another requirement for membership was having only one parent. It could be by death, divorce, or abandonment, but all the members had only one living parent which is why my other friends such as Eddie Arnold were uninvited. The final rule was an age requirement. One had to be between the ages of nine and twelve. On a thirteenth birthday, the name was eliminated from his list.

This private club of Mr. Organ's was entirely of his making and his purpose (as near as I could determine) was to be a surrogate grandfather to as many kids as he could, taking them to places they might not otherwise be able to enjoy. Some of those places were, Central Park, The Bronx Zoo, The Museum Of Natural History, Coney Island. There were probably other destinations but these were the excursions I took with him. He alternated taking boys one week and girls the following week, doing it all summer long while we were on vacation from school.

He would send a postcard to the homes of the selected fifteen (more or less) children two weeks before the event. There were details of where we were going, what time to meet at the designated bus stop (Forest Avenue and Clove Road) and how much money to bring. The card also reminded us to bring a sack lunch and our parental permission note.

There were simple rules for maintaining membership in the exclusive club. He explained those rules carefully, explicitly, and if you broke any of them your name was eliminated from his list. Once, I sneaked a peek at the list of names he kept in the little spiral book he closeted in the inside pocket of his suit coat, a black, pin-striped suit with matching vest. There were dozens of names, some crossed out, all with little red-penciled checks next to them. The checks probably indicated when they had attended an outing. I'm sure he played no favorites from what I could observe in that cursory examination.

The rules were simple. We were expected to stay together (we didn't need to hold hands, however) and be silent when he asked us. This was an easy rule to follow because he allowed us to chatter and laugh like children until we entered say, a museum, or some like establishment. Then he would prompt us in the proper deportment. When we went on our various outings he would collect the signed release forms and check that everyone had the amount of money he deemed necessary for the day's event. It would include carfare, entrance fees (if any) and some cash for sodas and miscellaneous needs. I seem to recall needing less than a dollar, maybe sixty-five cents, for most of the trips. Coney Island was a bit more because of the rides. I'm not sure he would actually cut someone off if they were short of carfare. More than once I saw him reach into his own pocket to help some boy who had overspent his allowance before boarding the ferryboat home. In 1947 the bus, ferry and subway rides were all five cents.

His physical presence was abundant. He had the appearance of Santa Claus, a full-head of white hair flowing directly into a long white beard and substantial mustache. His ample girth was reminiscent of Santa as well, and with his height somewhat over six feet, he was an imposing presence to all of us small kids. I imagine he was imposing to anyone!

But his jovial nature was his defining feature.

Staten Island Folklore

He was soft-spoken and seemed to have a continual twinkle in his eyes. He laughed often and never teased anyone for fun. He also carried several magic tricks and a set of tumbling wooden "cards" that were connected by ribbons wrapped around them in such a way that he could keep them tumbling interminably. I was fascinated by those tumbling cards and much later in life I bought a set for myself. He entertained us often with the tricks and cards during the long bus and subway rides to wherever we were going. This gentle soul had infinite patience and I never heard him raise his voice in anger or command beyond what was needed to be heard. He taught us how to use the subway and the buses as well as teaching us about the value of parks and museums and zoos. What an education!

    I can still feel the excitement I felt listening to him tell us about a grizzly bear similar to the one we were looking at in the Museum of Natural History. He stood in front of the bear, all of us boys sitting on the floor in front of him, the seven-foot bear dwarfing even his own impressive size. He told us about a hunter who shot a bear but had succeeded in only wounding the grizzly in his left foreleg near the shoulder.

Staten Island Folklore

"The bear ran away and for days was sick because of the wound and the loss of blood. The foreleg became numb and useless. Finally, with his disabled limb more of a hindrance than help as it dragged uselessly at his side, the bear tore the useless leg off with his teeth and the claws of his good, right foreleg."

We sat there, mesmerized. The museum was quiet except for the voice of Mr. Organ.

"A year later, the hunter was back in the same spot in Montana, hunting bear again. He walked miles but never saw a bear. Finally, coming to a place near the edge of a cliff, with a beautiful view of the lush, green meadow below, the hunter rested his gun against a large rock and went to the edge of the cliff to sit and enjoy the beautiful view. Lost in the scenic beauty he didn't hear the bear come up behind him.

"Suddenly, he heard the bear growl with a voice as big as the view he was looking at. He jumped up and there was the bear...just as big as this bear right here," Mr. Organ said, pointing to the stuffed bear beside him, "and the bear had his good right arm raised just like this..." and Mr. Organ raised his arm in imitation of the bear. I remember trembling at the image he created.

"The man, knowing immediately that this must be

Staten Island Folklore

the bear he had shot last year, looked to his gun, but the bear was squarely between him and it. There was nothing he could do. Nothing. He knew he was going to be killed ... if not by the bear's slashing claws, then by the fall from the cliff, for surely he would be knocked off the two hundred-foot high cliff."
Mr. Organ paused again. He was a master story-teller. Even today, I envy his ability to keep fifteen nine and ten-year-olds in rapt, silent attention for such a length of time. "Then, the bear growled again, dropped to the ground, turned, and walked away."
The story-teller waited for our sigh, a sigh of gratitude that the bear had spared the hunter. After a moment, he went on. "The hunter then went for his rifle...and threw it over the cliff! He never hunted again in appreciation for the forgiveness that bear had showed him." And Mr. Organ moved away from the bear on to the next exhibit, a giant blue whale, and another story. I remember these stories fifty years later. Is it any wonder I remember Mr. Organ? What a man!
The sad part is that the man could not, today, do what he did then. Our parents never even met the man. I suppose some might have, but his reputation was such that by the time he came into

Staten Island Folklore

my life, none seemed to have done so. He was one of a kind. He did what can never be done again. I can only be thankful that I was lucky enough to have known him when I did.

~ story submitted by Don Dolan

Here is an email from another visitor to my website that remembers Mr. Organ

Hi John...I'd be glad to tell you what I can remember about Mr Organ..A very nice old gent that hung around Westerleigh and he loved children. He would sit in the park near PS 30 and carve little miniature hand baskets out of walnut shells and give them to the kids...yeah we still had walnuts at the time (throughout the 30s and 40s, He knew of a field where he would cut walking sticks..he would strip the bark off of them and give them to the children...some of us knew that it was easy to cut one to length, hollow it out, and make pea shooters out of them.

During his hey day he would take small groups of children to various parks, exhibits, the S.I. Zoo and even to Coney Island, the Museum of Natural History and Central Park. I never saw

Staten Island Folklore

him without the same black suit, black vest and jacket and straw hat (Most of this took place in the warm part of the year) I never heard anyone talk about where he lived,if he had a family or an other details, and by the years around 1947 I went off to Port Richmond High School and don't know how long he kept it up. He was always totally proper, and parents apparently trusted him enough to let their children go on trips with him...I tend to think of his as a wonderful old man who loved children but probably had none of his own

I am sure that there are others my age (76 from Westerleigh, P.S. 30 that could tell you a lot more. I have lost addresses and forgotten names but it might be easy to check with the records people at P.S. 30 for the years around the late 30s , 40s and early fifties

A note from the Author . . . .
This story may raise a few eyebrows among all the parents that read this book, but believe me, I have read it over dozens of times, have heard from a few people who knew of this man and my feeling about it is just as Don states in the

Staten Island Folklore

opening, Mr. Organ was just being a surrogate grandfather.

Remember, the year was 1947, when times and attitudes were much different then now. Look at it this way, we all remember the total trust our parents had in the leaders of the church, our parents would never think twice about leaving us kids in the care of the clergy, can you say that these days?

After researching surrogate grandfathers, I found out there is a huge calling for them in other countries and there aren't enough elderly to fill the need. Just think about it, this Mr. Organ could have been childless, could have lost a child or maybe something all humans need, and that is the need to be needed.

Staten Island Folklore

Staten Island Folklore

Staten Island Folklore

Willie Sutton

Famous bank robber Willie Sutton settled on Staten Island after escaping from Holmesburg prison, Philadelphia in 1947. He hid out on Staten Island for months while the cops hunted him down
~ from The Saturday Evening Post June 9, 1951

Staten Island Folklore

Under the name of Eddie Lynch, he worked as a porter in the Farm Colony Hospital (across the road from Seaview Hospital) for $90.00 a month. After Willie crunched out of the Pennsylvania prison in February 1947, he'd come to Staten Island where he'd spent three whole years scrubbing floors in his hospital job, meanwhile living quietly with a landlady, Mary Corbett, on Kimball Avenue in Castleton Corners and going to church with her and helping her tend her crocuses. Sutton left Staten Island quickly when his landlady recognized him from a wanted poster. He enjoyed two more years of freedom living in Brooklyn, where his new landlady was blind, until a salesman spotted him and turned him in to the police.

Willie Sutton was sentenced to 30 years in prison and the guy, named Shuster, who turned him in, was shot and killed three weeks later.

Sutton spent 37 of his 79 years of life in prison and died in 1980.

Staten Island Folklore

Throughout much of this period, he was very patiently observing the daily routines at the Manufacturers Trust Co., 47-11 Queens Blvd., Sunnyside, Queens, getting to know exactly what the guards did when. Accordingly, things went like perfect clockwork when Willie and several pals hit the bank for $63,933 one morning in March 1950. After which Willie unobtrusively took the IRT and the ferry and the No. 111 bus back to Kimball Avenue.

In Willie's words - "These young kids, they don't believe in hard work," he grumbled. "All these kids want to do is run into a bank, grab the

money and run out."
Newspaper headline -
Fugitive's Landlady Held in $50,000 Bail
The Washington Post
- Washington, D.C. Mar 26, 1950
A Staten Island woman who rented a room to Willie Sutton, bank robber and jail breaker, until four weeks ago was held in $50,000 bail today as a material witness in the $64,000 robbery of a bank in Sunnyside, Long Island, on March 9.

On March 28th, Willie Sutton was back in the headlines when the Star-Journal told its readers that his landlady was being questioned in the office of the Queens District Attorney in Long Island City. Sutton, who had escaped from jail in Pennsylvania in 1947, had recently spent several months on Staten Island working as a porter in a home for the elderly indigent. The Star--Journal reported that his landlady, Mary Corbett, was "being held on $50,000 bail as a material witness. It was learned today that Mary, who rented a room to Willie for seven months, had her bags packed when detectives picked her up."

According to the Star-Journal reporter, "the last time she saw Willie, Mary said, was on March

9th, the day after the robbery. She knew him only as Edward Lynch, she said. When she saw photos of Sutton in the newspapers after the hold-up." She asked Lynch about it. He told they were photos of his half-brother, who was "always getting me into trouble." Two hours later, she told detectives, he put $700 on the kitchen table and left."

The Star-Journal revealed that "Miss Corbett told police that she and Sutton watched the 1949 Saint Patrick's Day parade on Fifth Avenue at a time when the bandit was being sought all over the country." Sutton would not be captured until 1952, when a sharp-eyed 24-year-old tailor named Arnold Schuster recognized him on the subway. "Slick Willie" was tried and convicted for the robbery of the Manufacturer's Trust Co. Bank at the Queens County Courthouse in Long Island City. Popular sympathy for Sutton evaporated when Schuster was shot dead near his home in Brooklyn. It was later revealed that, unknown to Sutton, mob boss Albert Anastasia, who hated informers, had ordered the hit on Schuster.

Staten Island Folklore

Staten Island Folklore

"Mind the Light, Kate"

Staten Island Folklore

The most famous occupant of New York Harbor is surely Lady Liberty, who first struck her now permanent pose in 1886, just three years after the second Robbins Reef Lighthouse was built. In the lighthouse community, Kate Walker, keeper of Robbins Reef for over thirty years, runs a close second to the torch-bearing statue that stands just over two miles north of the lighthouse.

To gain an appreciation for Kate Walker, you have to travel back to northern Germany, where she was born Katherine Gortler in 1848. After finishing school, she married Jacob Kaird. The couple's only child, also named Jacob, was only seven years old when his father died. Seeking a new life, Kate took Jacob to America, where she accepted a position waiting tables at a boarding house in Sandy Hook, New Jersey. It was here where she met John Walker, assistant keeper of the Sandy Hook Lighthouse.

Kate knew very little English and gladly accepted Walker's offer of free English lessons. The student-teacher relationship quickly converted into a romantic one, and the two soon married. Kate enjoyed her life at the lighthouse, where there was land for her to grow vegetables and flowers. However, this life was short-lived as

Staten Island Folklore

John was offered the position as keeper of the recently reconstructed Robbins Reef Lighthouse.

Kate Walker

"When I first came to Robbins Reef," Kate recalled, "the sight of the water, whichever way I looked, made me lonesome. I refused to unpack my trunks at first, but gradually, a little at a time, I unpacked. After a while they were all unpacked and I stayed on." John received an annual salary of $600, while Kate was paid $350 to serve as his assistant. The couple, along with their son and new daughter Mary, quickly adjusted to their home with a 360-degree harbor view.

Tragedy touched the station in 1886, when John contracted pneumonia. As he was being taken ashore to a hospital, his parting words to his wife were "Mind the Light, Kate." John never returned to his family. For the second time in her life, Kate was a widow, but she carried on, motivated by the need to provide for her two children and fulfill her husband's wish. "Every morning when the sun comes up," Kate said, "I stand at the porthole and look towards his grave. Sometimes the hills are brown, sometimes they are green, sometimes they are white with snow. But always they bring a message from him, something I heard him say more often than anything else. Just three words: 'Mind the Light.' "

Staten Island Folklore

Although Kate had capably served as assistant keeper, the position of head keeper was only offered to her after two men had turned it down. Perhaps the Lighthouse Service doubted a petite, 4'10" woman, with two dependent children, could handle the job - and a tough job it was. Every day, Kate would row her children to school, record the weather in the logbook, polish the brass, and clean the lens. At night, she would wind up the weights multiple times to keep the fourth-order lens rotating, trim the wicks, refill the oil reservoir, and in times of fog, she would have to start up the steam engine in the basement to power the fog signal. As her son John matured, he started to help with the tasks and was later made an assistant.

Besides keeping the lighthouse in fine order, Kate also rowed out to assist distressed vessels and is credited with having saved fifty lives. Most of her rescues were fishermen whose boats were blown onto the reef by sudden storms. Kate observed, "Generally, they joke and laugh about it. I've never made up my mind whether they are courageous or stupid. Maybe they don't know how near they have come to their Maker, or perhaps they know and are not afraid. But I think that in the adventure they haven't realized how

Staten Island Folklore

near their souls have been to taking flight from the body."

After several years, Kate was more at home in the lighthouse than on land, and she was well acquainted with her nearest neighbors, the boats that frequently passed by her kitchen window. Recalling a trip she had made to New York City, Kate stated, "I am in fear from the time I leave the ferryboat. The street cars bewilder me and I am afraid of automobiles. Why, a fortune wouldn't tempt me to get into one of those things!" Upon hearing the noon whistle sound at a factory during one of her trips to the big city, she remarked, "If I hadn't known that the Richard B. Morse had been scrapped many years ago, I would have said that was that ship's whistle." It was later determined that the whistle was indeed from the Morse. After a scrap dealer purchased the ship, the whistle was salvaged and sold to the factory.

Kate served at the light until 1919, and then retired to nearby Staten Island where she could still keep an eye on the beacon. Even after her retirement and eventual passing in 1935 at the age of eighty-four, captains and harbor pilots still referred to the lighthouse as "Kate's Light."

When the Coast Guard assumed responsibility for Robbins Reef Lighthouse in 1939, a three-man crew lived in the lighthouse to perform the duties that not too many years prior had been carried out by the diminutive Kate Walker. In tribute to the heroic service offered by lighthouse keepers, each vessel in the Coast Guards fleet of fourteen, 175-foot Keeper Class Buoy Tenders is named after a keeper. The KATHERINE WALKER (WLM 552) was launched on September 14th, 1996, and appropriately, its homeport is in Bayonne, New Jersey, within sight of Robbins Reef Lighthouse.

Staten Island Folklore

Katie Walker adds rescuing people to her light keeping duties

At the sound of the gun and bugle on Governors Island, she climbed the stairs again to begin another night of work on the light. Despite her demanding duties as both light keeper and mother, Katie was an expert rower who managed to rescue a total of 50 people in the Robbins Reef light region, which was notorious for tidal whirlpools on the reef's outer rocky fringe. One of her most grateful patrons was a dog.

Katie Walker Rescues Scotty

One frigid winter day, a three-masted schooner labored against strong winds as it tried to pass Robbins Reef Light. It lurched, swayed, and went over on its beam ends on the reef landing. Katie let down the boat and rowed out to the schooner. Five men clung to it, and she helped them hoist themselves into the boat. As the last man tumbled in, he cried, "Where's Scotty?"

Hearing a feeble whine, Katie looked down into the water and spotted a shaggy brown dog. She caught the dog between the roars as he drifted by and hauled him into the boat.

"He crouched, shivering against my ankles. I'll never forget the look in his big brown eyes as he raised them to mine, "Katie recalled.

Katie and the sailors rowed against the wind for two hours before they could reach the lighthouse. Hugging Scotty inside her cloak, Katie hurried into her big kitchen. She sat him beside the stove and stoked the fire. Scotty fell over like a frozen corpse.

Katie rushed to the stove and poured some coffee from the pot she always kept hot during bad weather. She forced it down Scotty's throat, and he gasped and shivered. "Then his eyes opened and there was that same thankful look he had given me in the boat," Katie said.

Staten Island Folklore

Staten Island Folklore

The Manhattan Project

In 1945 the United States covert operation known as The Manhattan Project achieved its goal - to create the first atomic bomb.

Staten Island Folklore

Since its inception in 1939, scientists had struggled to find a way to harness the power of fission. Through the combined efforts of many, a test bomb known as "Fat Boy" was finally created. On July 16, 1945 in a desert in New Mexico the worlds first nuclear test, codenamed Trinity, was conducted and ushered in the Atomic Age. The Trinity test success led to the creation of two more atomic bombs that would be used in WWII.

On August 6, 1945 the American B-29 bomber known as the Enola Gay released the first atomic bomb to be used in warfare. The 9,000 pound bomb nicknamed "Little Boy" detonated in Hiroshima, Japan. "Little Boy's" explosion was catastrophic and resulted in 66,000 instantaneous deaths. Total vaporization from the blast measured one half a mile in diameter. Total destruction ranged one mile in diameter and serious blazes extended as far as three miles in diameter.

Can you believe that in our beloved island's past, 1,200 tons of high-grade uranium ore, that was used in the production of that bomb, was stored on Staten Island in the shadow of the Bayonne Bridge.

Staten Island Folklore

Staten Island Folklore

It was this very ore, stored on Richmond Terrace, that humans took up and transformed into an atomic weapon to be dropped on Hiroshima.

It was stored here from 1939 to 1942 on Richmond Terrace. A junkyard and truck-parking lot occupies the industrial site today. The Manhattan Project was the codename for a project conducted during World War II to develop the first atomic bombs, before the Germans or the Japanese. The project was led by the United States, and included participation from the United Kingdom and Canada.

The project's roots began in 1939 when at the urging of Leó Szilárd, Albert Einstein signed a letter to President Roosevelt expressing his concerns that Nazi Germany may be trying to develop nuclear weapons. The Manhattan Project, which began as a small research program that year, eventually employed more than 130,000 people and cost nearly $2 billion dollars ($22 billion in present day value). It resulted in the creation of several research and production sites whose construction and operations were secret.

In 1939, a ship carrying raw uranium ore from the Belgian Congo steamed into New York

Staten Island Folklore

Harbor. It bore left around Staten Island into the Kill van Kull and docked under the Bayonne Bridge.

Few people other than NYC Mayor Fiorello La Guardia knew it was there. Not even the Staten Island Borough President was included in the plan.

The uranium eventually was sent by train across the United States, destined for scientists developing the world's first atomic bomb in Los Alamos, New Mexico.

In 1939, Archer Daniels Midlands Co. agreed to use a portion of their linseed oil manufacturing property on Staten Island to store the 1,200 tons of high-grade uranium ore mined in what was then the Belgian Congo. The uranium, purchased from African Metals Corp., was to be used in building the atomic bomb. However, at some point (either during initial delivery or eventual shipment), uranium spilled on the waterfront property.

For three years, some 1,250 tons of the radioactive material was stored in 2,007 steel drums under the Bayonne Bridge off Richmond Terrace in Port Richmond.

The U.S. government bought the stockpile on Sept. 18, 1942, for the Manhattan Project - the super secret A-bomb program.

It is widely believed that the Manhattan Project's name was a code name. In fact, the project was named after Manhattan Island of New York City, as that was the location where many of its early operations were conducted. It is said that at least ten sites operated in Manhattan. The island was an ideal location because of its port facilities, the military presence, a large available work force, a population of expatriate European physicists, and Columbia University, a center of early nuclear research.

The area where it was stored was bounded by Richmond Terrace to the north, Nicholas Avenue to the east, John Street to the west and the now defunct North Shore Railroad to the south. After limited radiological testing in 1980 and 1992 detected low-level contamination from apparent leaks and spills, it was never cleaned up, just fenced off.

Since the half-life of uranium ranges from thousands to billions of years, the stuff is not going away anytime soon, but it poses no immediate public health risk, if left undisturbed.

Through the years, the site, which was never remediated, remained industrial. The link to the Manhattan Project was no more than urban legend until 1980, when the site was tested for radioactivity by representatives from the Oak Ridge National Laboratory, a Tennessee facility established as part of the Manhattan Project. The tests proved positive, but the report was swallowed by the U.S. Dept. of Energy, once known as the Atomic Energy Commission.

Twelve years later, in 1992, the New York State Department of Environmental Conservation conducted another assessment, this time of subsurface soil. It found the soil below the surface was far more radioactive than the surface samples studied by the energy department. Yet, for reasons as yet unknown, no action was taken.

Because the site is also located within a 100-year flood plain, the Environmental Protection Agency believes that, in the event of a flood, there would be "a high tendency" for the material to migrate into the adjacent Kill Van Kull and Newark Bay. Moreover, the agency's report states that although the area is currently fenced, trespassers coming either by land or water and site workers could "receive an unacceptable cancer risk under a conservative hypothetical risk assessment scenario."

Staten Island Folklore

The analysis is frightening enough, but the severe weather and increased flooding brought on by climate change makes it that much more terrifying.

The Environmental Protection Agency sent a letter to the energy department requesting that it reconsider the property for inclusion under its remedial action program. It also recommended that the energy department do another search for a responsible party – at this point, that would be either African Metals Corp. or Archer Daniels Midland. Finally, the agency stated that if the first two recommendations did not come to fruition, it would consider taking at least a limited action to further protect public health concerns at the site.

In 1999, the site across the street from the radioactive area was purchased by developers who wanted to rezone it as residential. As part of the rezoning, community members participated in the City's Uniform Land Use Review Process -- and the myth of the Manhattan Project was retold. That's when the North Shore Waterfront Conservancy, first heard about it. They questioned the wisdom of building hundreds of new homes in such an area.

Staten Island Folklore

The government rejected responsibility to include the site in a federal remediation program because it was privately owned during the time of the uranium storage.

Staten Island Folklore

Staten Island Folklore

The Great Bronze Column

The Eighth Wonder of the World
580 feet tall

Staten Island Folklore

Had this grand vision been realized, the first view of the New World to greet arriving immigrants arriving after 1913 would have been a 580 foot tall tribute to the American Indian.

At the entrance to New York Harbor, overlooking the Narrows from the heights of Staten Island and perched atop a seven-story pedestal, the mammoth figure of an Indian chief was to have been erected, his hand uplifted and two fingers extended in the "universal peace sign of the red man." Towering 165 feet above a sprawling complex of museums, libraries, and formal gardens, he would have been the nation's ultimate memorial to the "vanishing" North American Indian.

It was to be known in the years to come as "The Great Bronze Column of Staten Island." Between the volutes at the base of the capitol, running horizontally around the column, is the balustrade or viewing point of the Monument, 435 feet above the ground.

This point can be reached by a circular stairway or by the more modern elevator system.

It is interesting to note that this gigantic figure will be brought into human semblance through an entirely new method by the use of cement. In

Staten Island Folklore

forming the huge sections, the metal instead of being pounded into shape, according to the old, slow and exasperating process, will be pressed, bolted and anchored by an entirely new system of advanced ideas.

The figure according to present calculations is four feet higher than the Statue of Liberty ; the Column will be the highest column ever erected in the history of the world and the entire monument, which is a marvelous example of engineering, architecture and sculpture combined, will surpass in height any existing figure - monument ever erected.

The museum at the base of the shaft serves a dual purpose as a library and museum or hall of records for authentic Indian documents and historical data.

An assembly room has also been planned on the floor above.

The revenue from sight-seers and tourists will in time reach an amount sufficient to provide for the maintenance of the library and museum and the cost of operating expenses.

It is a great undertaking but with the assistance of the men of prominence now interested in this project, the completion of the monument is **assured** (or so they thought) and the world will be inspired by awe at this symbol of greatness erected to so great a country.

The museum building which forms the base of the monument is 50 feet high and will be of granite, properly embellished, with Entrance and Exit, properly lighted. There will be sufficient stack-room facilities for records and exhibits of the North American Indian and the collection will be under the supervision of men familiar with the subject and capable of overseeing this department.

The second story will be fitted as a place of assembly where conferences may be held relative to historical and Indian matters.

This bronze column is 401 feet high from the top of the museum to the base of the figure and will be constructed of steel girders, anchored in cement below the surface of the earth, and encircled by 45 sections of copper plate, one for each State of the Union. Two elevators will run to the base of the capital which is to be made in the form of a promenade.

The column will be surmounted by a beautiful ionic capital with leaded glass front, the two volutes acting as beacons for signaling ships or for transmitting signals to the surrounding country.

Staten Island Folklore

The top or roof as it were, to the great capital will be gilded in order to separate the flowing color where the capital meets the figure.

This figure will be 129 feet high from the feet to the top of head (24 feet higher than the Colossus of Rhodes) and will be constructed of steel armatures covered with copper plates properly reinforced.

There will be an entrance at each foot. The sightseer will also be able to ascend inside the bronze figure to the head, some 580 feet from the level of the ground. Resting places will be installed, one at the waist, the other at the shoulders.

The elevation of this great monument, plus the height of the position where it may perhaps rest, will be in the neighborhood of 960 feet above sea-level. Which is the highest point on the Atlantic coast between Maine and Mexico.

The site on which the monument will rest is to be chosen by the Commission

The cost of this work will reach approximately $650,000.

This flamboyant scheme was gotten up by Rodman Wanamaker, the son of John Wanamaker, who had built a Philadelphia men's clothing store into one of America's largest retail empires. Blessed with the bounty of this heritage, the younger Wanamaker acquired a formidable reputation as a patron of the arts, an aviation enthusiast, and an American Indian buff of considerable dimensions. Convinced, as was much of his generation, that the Indian was fast approaching extinction, he had financed expeditions to collect facts, artifacts, and movie film of the doomed people before they slipped into oblivion. Then, at a dinner party in 1909 at New York City's fashionable Sherry's restaurant, with such notables as Buffalo Bill in attendance, he proposed the construction of a great monument to the Indian in New York Harbor.

The site finally selected was the front portion of Fort Tompkins, the highest rampart within the Fort Wadsworth complex on Staten Island (the same structure that today houses a military museum). And so it was that on Washington's bdirthday, 1913, President William Howard Taft, struggled up the steps of Fort Wadsworth for the dedication. On hand was an odd assortment of politicians, military officers, academicians, battle-garbed tribal chiefs, newspapermen, and movie cameramen hired by Wanamaker.

Staten Island Folklore

Indian Monument Dedication February 1913 Photo shows President William Howard Taft at the groundbreaking ceremony for the National American Indian Memorial (which was never built), Fort Wadsworth, Staten Island, New York

Wanamaker's monument never got beyond the paper it was drawn on. The bronze tablet that had been implanted in 1913 mysteriously vanished, never to be seen again. The concept was resurrected briefly in 1936 as a potential Work Projects Administration program, but died away, then arose again a decade later when a proposed memorial to World War II veterans from Staten Island had to be shifted from Fort Tompkins because of the Indian monument's previous claim; this brief surge of interest died also.

Staten Island Folklore

Comparative Heights of Famous Monuments

- Eifel Tower, Paris, France
  984 ft.

- Bronze Column Staten Island, N. Y.
  580 ft.

- Washington Monument, Washington DC
  555 ft.

- The Great Pyramid, 12 miles from Cairo,
  543 ft.

- Statue of Liberty, N. Y. Harbor
  305 ft.

- Bunker Hill Monument, Boston, Mass.
  221 ft.

- Colossus of Rhodes, Harbor of Rhodes
  105 ft.

Too bad it never happened.
The planned locations were Pavilion Hill in St. George or Fort Wadsworth.

Staten Island Folklore

Staten Island Folklore

The Legend of Cropsey

Staten Island Folklore

Every town has urban legends – many are just spooky stories started by parents to keep children from wandering off and exploring dark and unknown places. But what happens when those legends become more like reality? When five children go missing on Staten Island, residents realize that the scary tales of their youth may be based in fact.

The legend of "Cropsey" - the escaped mental patient who lived in the abandoned tunnels of the Willowbrook mental hospital and came out at night to snatch young kids off the streets of Staten Island. "Cropsey" remained just that, an urban legend, a kidnapper who reportedly stalked the tunnels and halls of an abandoned Staten Island mental institution, was nothing more than a hook-handed, axe-wielding urban legend until 1987, when the real body of a 13-year-old girl with Down syndrome was found buried in a shallow grave on the grounds of Willowbrook. Investigators soon linked this case to four other missing children cases in the area - none of whom had been found.

'Cropsey' was born Frank Rushan March 11, 1944. He changed his name to Andre Rand in 1968 after working as a janitor at the Willowbrook mental institution.

May 25, 1969 - Rand had his first brush with the law when he abducted and tried to have sex with a 9-year-old girl. He was caught before the assault occurred and served 16 months for attempted sexual assault.

1979 - Accused of raping a young woman and a 15-year-old girl but since neither pressed charges, Rand was never indicted.

1981 - Tried to entice a 9-year-old girl into his car with candy. When she refused, he followed her home. She hid from him and no charges were filed. Another little girl, Holly Ann Hughes, was not so lucky. She disappeared in the summer of 1981 and has never been found.

1983 - Drove to the Staten Island YMCA and picked up a group of 11 children, bought them White Castle and took them to the Newark Airport to watch the planes. Though no children were harmed, Rand was charged with unlawful imprisonment for which he served 10 months in jail.

Staten Island Folklore

10-year-old Tiahease Tiawanna Jackson disappeared on August 14th, 1983.

1987 - 12-year-old Jennifer Schweiger, a little girl with Down's Syndrome, disappeared on July 9th, 1987. A month later, her nude body was found in a shallow grave near Rand's campsite on the grounds of Willowbrook State Mental Facility.

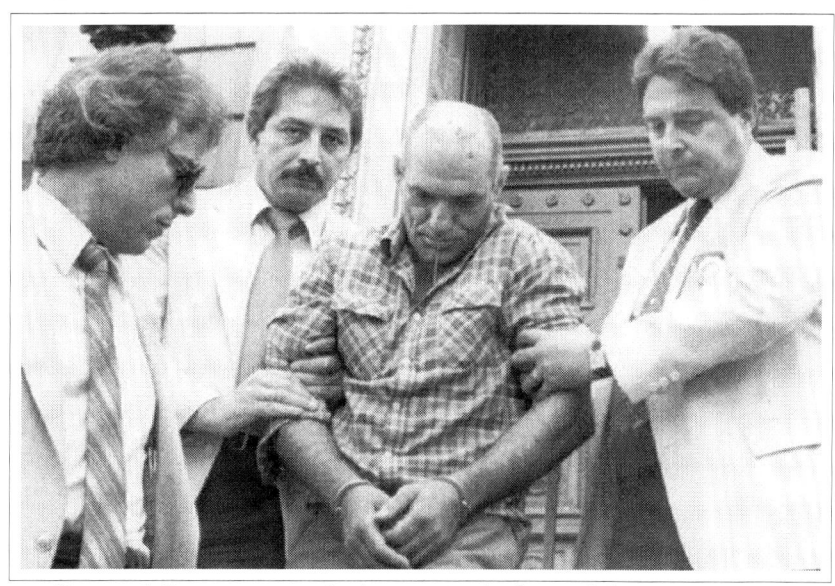

One of the unusual characteristics of Andre Rand is that most of his victims were usually random strangers. Most kidnappers either know or are at least somewhat acquainted with their victims.

Staten Island Folklore

In 2002, Andre Rand was found guilty of the 1987 kidnapping of Jennifer Schweiger and given 25 years to life in prison.

In 2004, Rand was indicted in the 1983 disappearance of 10-year-old Tiahease Tiawanna Jackson.

The bodies of four people are still unaccounted for including Alice Pereia, Holly Ann Hughes, Tiahease Tiawanna Jackson & Henry Gafforio. Audrey Lyn Nergenberg, an eighteen-year-old who disappeared in 1977, is also believed to be linked to Rand.

Staten Island Folklore

Staten Island Folklore

Who Invented the Telephone?

Antonio Meucci
1808 - 1889

Antonio Meucci filed a patent caveat for a telephone device in December of 1871. Patent caveats according to law were "a description of an invention, intended to be patented, lodged in the patent office before the patent was applied for, and operated as a bar to the issue of any patent to any other person regarding the same invention." Caveats lasted one year and were renewable. Patent caveats were much less costly than a full patent application and required a less detailed description of the invention. The U.S. Patent Office would note the subject matter of the caveat (no longer issued) and hold it in confidentiality. If within the year another inventor filed a patent application for a similar invention, the Patent Office notified the holder of the caveat, who then had three months to submit a formal application. Antonio Meucci did not renew his caveat after 1874 and Alexander Graham Bell was granted a patent in March of 1876. It should be pointed out that a caveat does not guarantee that a patent will be granted, or what the scope of that patent will be. Antonio Meucci was granted fourteen patents for other inventions, which leads me to question the reasons that Meucci did not file a patent application for his telephone, when patents were granted to him in 1872, 1873, 1875, and 1876.

In 2001 the House of Representative passed a resolution #269, expressing the sense of the House of Representatives to honor the life and

Staten Island Folklore

achievements of 19th Century Italian-American inventor Antonio Meucci, and his work in the invention of the telephone.

Whereas Antonio Meucci, the great Italian inventor, had a career that was both extraordinary and tragic;

Whereas, upon immigrating to New York, Meucci continued to work with ceaseless vigor on a project he had begun in Havana, Cuba, an invention he later called the `teletrofono', involving electronic communications;

Whereas Meucci set up a rudimentary communications link in his Staten Island home that connected the basement with the first floor, and later, when his wife began to suffer from crippling arthritis, he created a permanent link between his lab and his wife's second floor bedroom;

Whereas, having exhausted most of his life's savings in pursuing his work, Meucci was unable to commercialize his invention, though he demonstrated his invention in 1860 and had a description of it published in New York's Italian language newspaper;

Whereas Meucci never learned English well enough to navigate the complex American business community;

Staten Island Folklore

Whereas Meucci was unable to raise sufficient funds to pay his way through the patent application process, and thus had to settle for a caveat, a one year renewable notice of an impending patent, which was first filed on December 28, 1871;

Whereas Meucci later learned that the Western Union affiliate laboratory reportedly lost his working models, and Meucci, who at this point was living on public assistance, was unable to renew the caveat after 1874;

Whereas in March 1876, Alexander Graham Bell, who conducted experiments in the same laboratory where Meucci's materials had been stored, was granted a patent and was thereafter credited with inventing the telephone;

Whereas on January 13, 1887, the Government of the United States moved to annul the patent issued to Bell on the grounds of fraud and misrepresentation, a case that the Supreme Court found viable and remanded for trial;

Whereas Meucci died in October 1889, the Bell patent expired in January 1893, and the case was discontinued as moot without ever reaching the underlying issue of the true inventor of the telephone entitled to the patent; and

Whereas if Meucci had been able to pay the

Staten Island Folklore

$10 fee to maintain the caveat after 1874, no patent could have been issued to Bell: Now, therefore, be it;

Resolved, That it is the sense of the House of Representatives that the life and achievements of Antonio Meucci should be recognized, and his work in the invention of the telephone should be acknowledged.

Staten Island Folklore

Staten Island Folklore

Sunday Bomber

The ferry seats after the bombing

Staten Island Folklore

Think todays terror alerts, warnings and bombings are something new?, think again. In October of 1960 a serial attacker, known as the Sunday Bomber, left bombs in a subway car, a subway station, the Staten Island Ferry and public buildings, killing one person and injuring fifty-one.

This story was most likely overshadowed by the terrible air crash of December of the same year. But this was a huge disaster in its own right. That bomber was never caught.

The bombing of the Staten Island Ferry, Knickerbocker, was the fourth bombing of the month. On October 2nd a bomb went off in Duffy Square near Times Square, injuring six people. The New York Public Library at 5th Avenue and 42nd Street, was the sight of the second bombing on October 9th. No one was hurt in that explosion. On Columbus day, an explosion in a photographic booth in a Times Square subway station injured thirty-two people.

Then on October 24th, at approximately 5:30 pm, the Knickerbocker ferry left Manhattan, heading for Staten Island, when minutes into the journey a shattering explosion was heard by the Captain. His first concern was that of injured passengers or the possibility of a sinking ferry.

Luckily for all on board, no one was hurt. The bomb was planted under a seat, among the life

Staten Island Folklore

preservers, near the womans room. It is believed that the bomber had planted the explosive about fifteen minutes before the ferry docked at South Ferry and that the bomber departed the ferry before its return trip to Staten Island.

Staten Island Folklore

Staten Island Folklore

Staten Island Moonshine

(not a Staten Island photo)

Staten Island Folklore

Even though Staten Island was home to a revolutionary community called Prohibition Park in Westerleigh, during the 19th century, that was an all dry neighborhood which, for ten years, hosted many temperance and other progressive speakers, the island was not immune to the evils of liquor.

Three such stories follow . . . .

In 1904

Philip Gold - a court interpreter turned moonshiner.
Philip, a highly educated man who stood six foot three inches tall was enticed into the moonshine business with promises of riches. A husband and father of two, Mr Gold wept like a child when he was charged with operating a moonshine still out of his home in South Beach, Staten Island.

    In searching the home the Revenue Agents say that they found a hundred gallon twin copper still and approximately six hundred gallons of yeast and sugar mash.

    Gold, who was on vacation from his court interpreter job in Boston, was convinced by people here that there was lots of money to be made in the scheme.

When questioned in the Commissioners office he broke down and admitted guilt. He stated that he didn't care for himself, but that it was the disgrace he had brought upon his family that upset him.

Born in Egypt, Gold said that he could read and write eight languages and speak fluently in ten. His remarkable story was confirmed. When he was locked up, he could not even post bail, for all of his money was invested in the copper still, which will be destroyed by the revenue officers.

In 1922

A giant still that was approximately five hundred gallons in size was discovered at Jackson Avenue near Fort Wadsworth.

A fire started by an explosion of the still caused $10,000 in damage. In the corner of the basement stood a second, smaller still, unharmed by the blast.

The explosion, initially was a mystery, until a police inspector, knowing that moonshine has been distributed from the Fort Wadsworth area, decided to investigate.

Detectives reported to the inspector, after entering the burned out wreck, that they had discovered the remains of a five hundred gallon still. A further search found another, smaller still, which was 300 gallons in size and completely undisturbed.

Also discovered were a large quantity of mash, 256 bottles of moonshine and a large quantity of alcohol.

The damage caused by the explosion, which could be heard for some distance, included an entire rear wall and one of the side walls.

Upon further investigation, it was found that the owners of the operation had tapped into the water and gas lines, in order to save money and also in an effort to prevent discovery.

Police had speculated that the still in the area was getting ready for the opening of the South Beach Resorts, in an attempt to quench the thirst of many a beach goer.

Staten Island Folklore

In 1954

This is the Rossville House taken by Paul Sharrott

In Sept 1954 in Rossville the Treasury Dept shut down a major moonshine operation, at the time it cost the operators $20,000 to build and it was capable of producing 1,000 gallons of alcohol in 12 hours. The still was built into a two-story house and had 18 inch copper tubes running from the basement to the attic, the operation was so big that the first stage of the mash was in a two car garage which had three vats each capable of holding 8,000 gallons of mash, this was then pumped underground from the garage to the house which contained the still.

The Staten Islander who was involved and owned the property on Arthur Kill Road was Joseph Nemeth, 51 years old. He was a cesspool cleaner by trade. The stills were located on his property in a run down house behind his own home. Nemeth was involved in the operation with three other people, all of whom resided in New Jersey.

The still was so huge and the Treasury Agents were so impressed with it that they postponed dismantling it until they could hold classes there.

New agents in the department, many of whom had never seen a still, attended classes in the dilapidated house and garage.

The Staten Islander, who led me to the 1954 story, had a memory jolt when I showed him what I had uncovered on this still story.

Staten Island Folklore

In an email to me he relates more of what he remembers about this story.

This is what he wrote. . . .

John,

I just read your article about the still in Rossville on the Staten Island Forum. I first found the old house at about the age of nine which was 1955. I lived on Claypit Road and found it one day while exploring the woods looking for arrow points. The house was a two story building with a basement and attic. The still was huge and sat on the basement floor to the right side of the stairway as you entered the front door from the front porch. All the rooms to the left of the staircase were intact but empty. The house was at the end of a very short dirt road leading up from Arthur Kill Road. The floor was strewn with lots of sacks of grain, which I suppose were used in the process of making moonshine. By the way, the still was riddled with machine gun holes. I know it was machine gun holes because of the way the holes were in lines and sort of up and down like it was sprayed to render it useless.

As you proceeded up the stairs there was a small room to the left. In that room there was a

Staten Island Folklore

large hole in the ceiling leading to the attic. This hole was chopped into the ceiling, not a normal attic access. The attic was chock full of what looked like all the original furniture and items from the original house. There were kerosene lamps, books, tables etc. I specifically remember a stack of farmers almanacs dated about 1874 with the name S.G.Winant imprinted on them. As you know, the area was named Winant as I remember it as a child. I always assumed that the house was originally owned by S.G.Winant who was a prominent figure in the area at the time and I always wondered just how much he was involved, if any, with that old still.

At the top of the stairs there was a window leading out to the roof of the back porch. The back porch had lots of junk in it including a player piano and many many piano rolls, all weather beaten because the roof was shot. In the back yard there was a large stable like structure which had either collapsed or was flattened on purpose. I crawled under it one day (remember, I was an inquisitive kid) and it was also full of household items like furniture, dishes, etc.

I went back to that area many times as a child to explore and to this day I clearly remember that giant still with all the bullet holes in it and I used

Staten Island Folklore

to wonder how many gangsters the "G" men killed in that old haunted house.

Late one night years later when the old house was just about falling down my older brother and I were heading through the woods on the way to, well somewhere, and as we were passing it my brother looked into a window, when all of a sudden an old woman in white with long stringy white hair and a kerosene lantern appeared at the window. Needless to say we made it home in record time and never went back. True story.

Well John, these are just some of the recollections of a child pioneer/explorer of those old woods between Arthur Kill Road, Claypit Road and Sharrotts Road.

~ memories of Paul A Sharrott

Staten Island Folklore

Staten Island Folklore

The Buried Guineas

It was some time between the cessation of actual hostilities and the evacuation of New York, Long Island and Staten Island by the British, that the following incident is said to have occurred.

There were many ships of war lying at anchor in various parts of the harbor; there were some, which laid in, and even beyond the Narrows, and these were anchored as near the shores of Long Island and Staten Island, as could safely be done. This was a convenient way to have easy access to the land in all conditions of the weather, in order that the officers might obtain supplies from the farmers in the vicinity.

One day, a boy, about seventeen or eighteen, whose father was a relative of the narrator of this story, was in search of some stray cattle in the woods near the water. While on his hunt he spotted a ship's boat with two sailors, approaching the shore. Figuring he might as well keep out of their view in such a solitary place, he concealed himself behind a large tree; he watched them land, and while one of them stayed behind to tend to the boat, the other, with basket in hand, entered the woods.

After having proceeded a short distance, until he was out of sight of his boat companion, and hopefully everyone else, he took off his coat, knelt down at the foot of a large tree and began to dig.

With a tool resembling a mason's trowel he dug a hole in the earth, partly under a large root, and then proceeded to buried something therein. Carefully, he filled the hole again with earth and laid a large flat stone upon it.

Having accomplished his purpose, whatever it might have been, he rose to his feet and took a long, slow look around then proceeded on his way.

The youth kept in his place of hiding for two long hours, when he spotted the sailor returning with his basket, apparently filled with vegetables. The sailor, on returning to his boat had passed the place where he had dug the hole, scrutinized it closely then continued on his way.

Assuring himself that the coast was clear, the young man went to the place, reopened the hole, and found therein a heavy canvas bag, evidently containing, as he judged from the sound, a quantity of money. Securing his prize, and not waiting to refill the hole, he hastened away and found another location of deposit, known only to himself.

A day or two after, posters were put up in every public place, offering a large reward for the recovery of three hundred guinea which were said to have been stolen from one of his majesty's ships and an additional reward for the capture of the thief. The incident caused much talk at the time but it was soon forgotten in all the excitement brought about with the declaration of peace and the preparation for the departure of the British from the country.

For nearly four years the young man kept his own secret, at which time he had attained the age of majority; and then, when he purchased a farm for himself, and paid for it, did, he first reveal, to his parents only, the manner in which he obtained his means.

Staten Island Folklore

Staten Island Folklore

Staten Island Folklore

Mr. Bang the Flower Man

His free bouquets brighten up ferry rides

Staten Island Folklore

AS A PRANK Bang leaves a lily in hand of a sle[ep]ing man. But flower dropped before man woke

Staten Island Folklore

For 40 years Charles Bang has been riding the Staten Island ferry. Nearly every day he has gotten aboard with an armful of flowers and walked around giving passengers cornflowers, lilies or whatever is in season.

Mr. Bang, 77 and a widower, grows the flowers in back of his Staten Island home. He gets up early every morning, before 7 AM to cut the blooms at their peak. "I would never give away flowers that were going to die soon", Mr. Bang says.

Staten Island Folklore

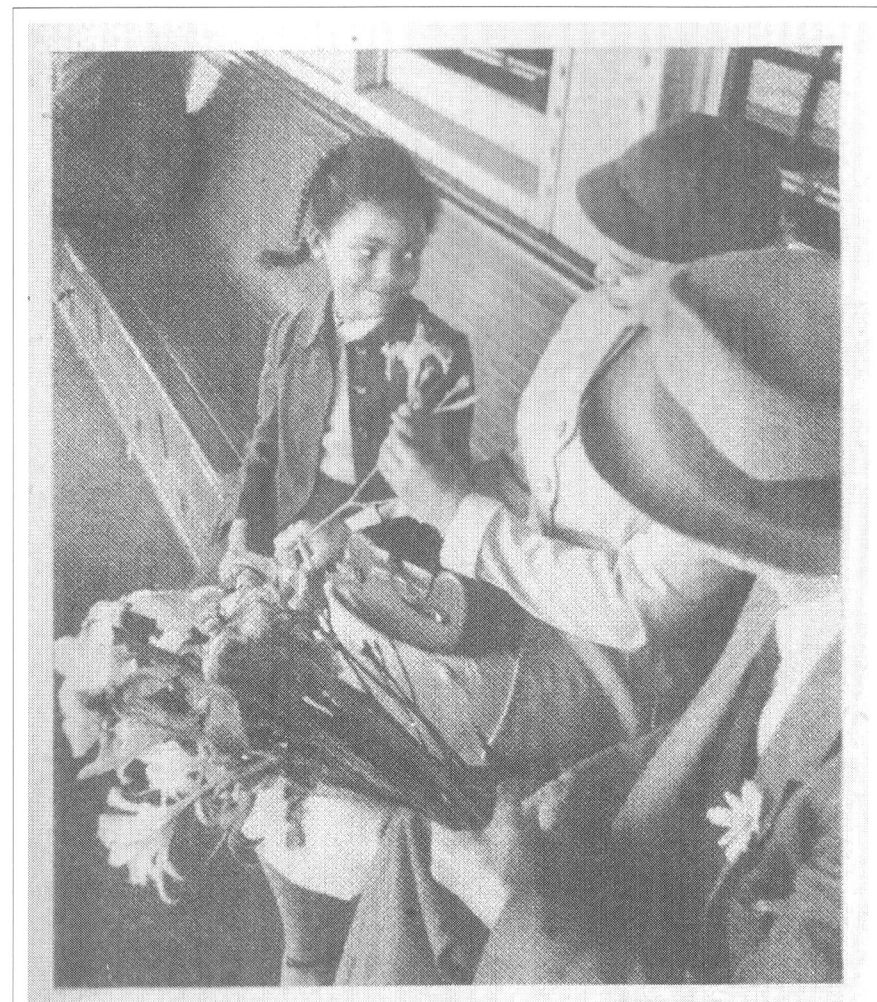

LITTLE GIRL, delighted by flower Mr. Bang gave her, hands it to aunt, who looks at it appraisingly.

Staten Island Folklore

Some days, the leftovers are passed out to the bus driver and the bus passengers

Staten Island Folklore

Many passengers, getting flowers for the first time, tend to shy away, being suspicious as most New Yorkers are. But his regulars, who call Mr. Bang Uncle Charlie, regard his beautiful floral gifts as part of a ferry rider's life.

SHOESHINE MAN gets sniff. Mr. Bang always gives him a large bouquet for his wife's birthday.

Staten Island Folklore

Mr. Bang dispenses most of his flowers on the ferry but saves a few to give to friends at the Fulton fish market as he walks through on the way to the cluttered salvage warehouse where he sells odds and ends.

~ from Life Magazine July 21, 1952

Staten Island Folklore

In conclusion let it be said that Staten Islanders may well be proud of their little island.

Where in the American continent is there a place more favored by nature than Staten Island? Its beautiful hills, commanding views of the ocean, its picturesque valleys, its magnificent forests, its pretty lakes, its sea shores, its climate, tempered by the proximity of the ocean, all combine to make it an ideal place for human habitation.

Those who live here love it, and the thoughts of those who have left it often turn with an affectionate memory to the happy days spent among its hills and forests.

~ written by Cornelius G Kolff 1918

Staten Island Folklore

Some Misc. Tales

Before the Revolution, superstition was rampant on the island. There was a haunted wood on the road to Old Town, and the 'Haunted Bridge" at the lower end of the island is still remembered. Then there was "Spook Swamp," and a house burned by the Indians, in which there was buried treasure so well guarded by a mad bull that it was never recovered.

Another road was frequented by a big black witch dog, which trotted along beside the horses of passing riders and bore a charmed life against pistol shots. A slave tried to kill it with a broadaxe, and swung the blade through its body. The dog howled just once, but the next minute was trotting beside the rider as strong and spooky as before. The slave fell in a fit.

It remained for New Springville to have a ghost the likes of which had never before been seen or heard of. It was nothing less than a child clad in garments of scarlet, which appeared by night and sometimes by day on top of a big rock, which used to stand opposite the Springville schoolhouse. It was not long before the good people of the village found a reason for the appearance of the child, and the story is a sad one.

One of the prettiest girls in the village became displeased with her parents and ran away from home. She came to New York, and from New York went to Albany. She loved a man who soon proved faithless by deserting her. She worked hard to support herself and her child, but finally gave up the struggle and returned home. Her parents received her with open arms, but not so the rest of the village. Polly, as she may be called, had been popular before when she had been but a maiden, but Polly, the mother, was impossible.

At first she stayed at home and the neighbors kept away. Then in church one day she made public confession of her sin. She thought that her old friends would forgive her. A neighbor was giving a flax bee (some kind of straw weaving party), and general invitations was sent to the young people of New Springville. No girl had more nimble fingers for the handling of flax than Polly, and she went to the "bee." She found a big room full of happy young people, hetchelling (combing the flax) and otherwise preparing it for the spinning wheel. They were laughing, telling jokes and teasing each other. After the work was finished they would dance. As Polly entered the door a silence fell upon the young people. Not one of them greeted her, though some of the boys would have done so gladly had they dared, for Polly was still prettier than any other New Springville woman. She sat down and began to work. The other girls complained to the head of the house and declared they would go home if Polly stayed. So the girl was driven out into the night, and with her went the chill of silence. The workers became merry and the flax bee was a success.

Late that night Polly took her child and stole out of her father's house, she was never seen again, and most people believed that she had thrown herself into the bay. It was winter before the vision of the scarlet child appeared to a party of young people going home from a spelling match. The night was well lighted by the moon and the snow was on the ground. There on a big rock at one side of the road stood the child, dressed in scarlet robes from head to foot. The girls were frightened and cried, for they feared that Polly's curse might fall on them.

Staten Island Folklore

Forgetful

A resident of Midland Beach, Captain Peter Lenderscarn, 63, of the barge Landlive, trying to secure his home rigged a double-barreled shotgun, pointing toward the front door of his bungalow, a string stretched from its trigger to the doorknob. Then he closed the bungalow, went voyaging on the barge Landlive. When he returned, he went to have a look at his bungalow. Forgetful, he went in by the front door, got his own leg blown off.

~ Time Magazine January 5, 1931

Staten Island Folklore

Come visit us on our website
www.statenislandhistory.com

Here's what people are saying about it.

- I learn something new each time I come back to this site. It is truly a labor of love and I thank you for that - Cheryleann, from Staten Island, New York

- Find myself looking at this site for hours - Gary from Allyn, Washington

- It's a great site! I'm enjoying my trip back home (it will always be home to me) – Linda, The Villages, Florida

- I love this site. I was trying to remember some of the places I went when I was a child and they were listed on your site – Susan, from St. Johnsbury, Vermont

- I was born and raised on Staten Island and love, love, love this web site. I will always be a native Staten Islander and hate to see how much the Island has changed. It certainly brings back

Staten Island Folklore

many fantastic memories of the Island and why I loved it so. Thanks for the labor of love! - Eugene, from Treasure Island, Florida

- Memories, memories and more memories. Can't stop smiling – Christine, from Walterboro, South Carolina

- Wonderful, brings back fond memories of the greatest place in the world to grow up – Richard, from Pittsburgh, Pennsylvania

- Great site, I come back to it every few weeks – Tommy, from Staten Island, New York

- This has made my day. I was born on Staten Island and lived there for 45 years before moving to Montana – Kristine, from Whitefish, Montana

- Great site. Have been coming here for a few years now and am enjoying all the additions you have made it it – Donald, from West Melbourne, Florida

- You brought tears to my eyes. Wonderful memories – Derba, from Branchburg, New Jersey

Staten Island Folklore

- This is so cool I can not wait to show my parents this site – Colleen, from Hudson Falls, New York

- The site is terrific and brings back so many memories. Please keep it alive so everyone can see how beautiful the island was - Ruth - from Thornton, Colorado

- I enjoy every word of this website – Jorge, from Santiago, Chile, South America

- Long overdue and a great website to recall your heritage – Edward, from Richmond Hill, Georgia

- Love this walk down the Memory Lane called Staten Island – Karen, from San Antonio, Texas

- Wonderful! I am longing for the old Island I knew and loved! - Anne, from Port Jervis, New York

- I cannot believe the amount of time and energy put into this site. Wonderful! - Gary, from Staten Island, New York

Staten Island Folklore

*If you enjoyed this book . . .
check out my second book*
"Famous People from Staten Island"

It contains photos and bios of over 120 people who at one time in their lives spent time on Staten Island. Some were born and raised here, some moved here, some worked here and some were educated here, but they all share a connection to our beloved Island.

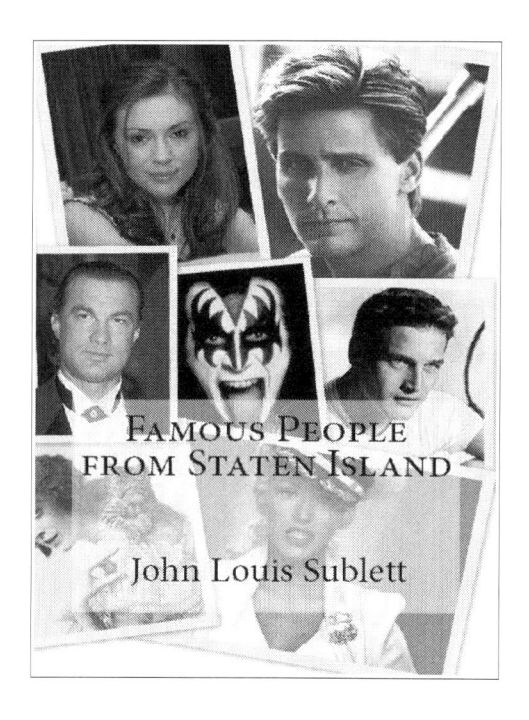

Staten Island Folklore

Or my very first book . . .

"Staten Island: A Walk Down Memory Lane"

Staten Island Folklore

About the book . . . .

Were there really four airports here? Was the Staten Island Airport shut down each night to ensure no peril to the patrons of the drive-in theater? Did rides and trolleys really exist on the South Beach - Midland Beach Boardwalk?

Were there restaurants with a huge hot dog on its roof or one built like a chuck wagon, a jolly trolley or a windmill. Were farms prevalent on the Island and did wildlife roam our backyards? Can it be that there were two movie theaters on New Dorp Lane? Were the beaches so clean that you actually paid to use them? Was fresh milk and bread actually delivered to our front door? Did Santa really ride the Christmas Train and stop at Jersey Street and Richmond Terrace and give out presents to the kids? Was there really a home for orphaned kids (Mount Loretto) (where once a month my mother promised to check me into)? In the 1930's, which of Staten Island's best known restaurateurs, bought a house across the street from his famous restaurant and built a 200-foot

Staten Island Folklore

tunnel between the house and the restaurant so that he could safely carry the day's receipts from the restaurant to his home. Did such rock legends, like the Allman Brothers, Vanilla Fudge, Alice Cooper, Black Sabbath and the Kinks really play the Island? Did John F Kennedy, sip coffee at the St. George ferry terminal? Can you believe that a famous Island milk company resorted to rowboats to delivery milk to areas from Oakwood to Midland Beach during some of the worst storms to every hit that area? These were some of the many questions I had as my interest in Staten Islands past grew. In recent years I have come across so much information about our Island's rich and diverse past, that I wanted to share with all Native Islanders and people who have called the Island home. But I did not want this to be another history book on Staten Island, though; at times it may look that way. I will not go into details about the British occupation of Staten Island for seven years, or the draft riots during the civil war, or the burning down of the Quarantine Station. I will try my best to make this a lighthearted look at memories that we have of a place that was and is still close to our hearts. I will try my best to make you say, "Wow, I remember that". . . .

Staten Island Folklore

Staten Island Folklore

Made in the USA
Charleston, SC
02 July 2011